James R. Wood received his B.D.
from Yale University and his Ph.D.
from Vanderbilt University. He is a
professor in the Department of
Sociology at Indiana University.
With David Knoke, he is the author
of Organized for Action:
Commitment in Voluntary
Associations.

# Leadership in Voluntary Organizations

# Leadership in Voluntary Organizations

## The Controversy over Social Action in Protestant Churches

James R. Wood

Rutgers University Press

New Brunswick, New Jersey

Library of Congress Cataloging in Publication Data

    Wood, James R    1933–
      Leadership in voluntary organizations.

      Bibliography: p.
      Includes index.
      1. Leadership.  2. Voluntarism.  3. Christian
leadership—Case studies.  I. Title.
HM146.W66      303.3′4      80–28837
ISBN 0–8135–0920–3

*For Myriam*

# Contents

# Figures and Tables

# *Preface*

This essay on leadership disputes Robert Michels's thesis that organization necessarily leads to oligarchy and its corollary that leaders cannot legitimately act counter to majority will. A study of local churches serves as an empirical basis for theoretical reflections on legitimacy in voluntary organizations. The central empirical question is: Was it legitimate for mainline Protestant leaders to involve their churches in social action opposed by the majority of their members? Michels's approach assumes a priori that such behavior by leaders is illegitimate and is explained by selfish interests. Drawing on a number of theorists, especially Max Weber, I argue that this assumption is at best simplistic and in some important respects demonstrably false.

The study of leadership in churches has many implications for other types of organizations, especially other value-fostering, voluntary organizations. Much of the research on organizations has addressed the problem of leaders' control, but most has been concerned with economic organizations. Yet the problem of control is especially interesting and, when the organization's values have been challenged, particularly acute in voluntary organizations. Because voluntary organizations cannot offer economic incentives, they provide a fruitful setting for studying noneconomic bases of control that are less apparent, though quite important, in economic organizations. The behavior from members that voluntary organizations most often need is simply the willingness to be counted as members and to make financial contributions so that the organization can carry out programs not dependent on direct member participation or can make pronouncements claiming the backing of a substantial number of people. With regard to at least some goals, this statement holds not only for religious denominations but also for such organizations as health and welfare associations, scientific and professional societies, social action groups, veterans' and patriotic organizations, fraternal orders, and labor unions. In such voluntary organizations effective strategies for securing participation from members may differ substantially from those appropriate in economic organizations. Especially when leaders face issues that divide the membership, such as racial justice and economic opportunity, they may need to pay close attention to establishing their legitimacy as leaders.

# *Acknowledgments*

Many people have contributed to the writing of this book. I am grateful to the late James D. Thompson, who as a scholar encouraged my work and as a person enriched my life. Mayer N. Zald has profoundly influenced my work through his lectures and published works, our numerous discussions, and his personal example. This book has benefited from critical comments by James Beckford, Jere Cohen, Jeffrey Hadden, Richard Hall, Paul Hirsch, J. Craig Jenkins, David Knoke, Delbert Miller, Charles Perrow, Marlie Wasserman, and Mayer Zald (who read an earlier draft), and from a debate with James L. Price concerning one of its central points. Consultants for the project included Elton F. Jackson (statistics), Irene Hess (sampling), Richard Myers (Indianapolis churches), Lois Downey (computer), and Carolyn J. Mullins (editorial). The expert contributions of all these persons are gratefully acknowledged.

I owe gratitude to James G. Hougland, Susan M. Anderson, and Janice Kennedy for much of the detailed work that is necessary to carry out any survey project. Esther Stanton, along with James Hougland and Susan Anderson, shared with me the interviewing of the 58 ministers. The principal manuscript typists were Janice Kennedy and Jacquelyn Warriner.

Numerous organizational officials at the national and local levels and a far larger number of members of these organizations are to be commended for giving their time to a scientific effort when more than ever the general public seems hesitant to become involved in such endeavors. Financial support for the project came from the Institute of Social Research, Indiana University, from the National Science Foundation (Grant No.

GS-28387), and, principally, from the National Institutes of Mental Health (Grant No. MH22884). This support is gratefully acknowledged.

I want to thank Kathryn Rutland Wood and Victor Hugo Wood for teaching me that knowledge is worth the cost of effort expended and pleasures foregone. I also want to thank Lillette Wood and Paul Wood for their occasional slave labor and their continual encouragement. Finally, this book is dedicated to Myriam Revel-Wood who, though she has not read one word of it, kept me at my task by her incredible devotion to a more demanding career.

# Leadership in Voluntary Organizations

# 1

## Introduction: The Bases of Legitimate Leadership

I first read Robert Michels's *Political Parties* (1962) in the early 1960s, when the organizations I knew best were mainline Protestant denominations. I was struck by the extent to which generalizations based primarily on political parties and labor unions half a century earlier were useful in understanding contemporary churches. Implementation of fundamental values in churches requires centralization of control, and numerous resources—many of them described by Michels—are available to leaders maintaining that control. But Michels's description did not fit one important feature of the contemporary scene: national church leaders in the 1960s were not determined to maintain their organizations' numerical strength and their own positions of power at the cost of values that were basic to their organizations.

The Episcopal Church provides a dramatic case in point. The commitment of the national Episcopal leadership to racial integration is evident in many statements and policies, including the following:

> Our Church's position on racial inclusiveness within its own body and its responsibility for racial justice in society has been made clear on many occasions by the General Convention. But there is urgent need to demonstrate by specific actions what God has laid on us. Such actions must move beyond expressions of corporate penitence for our failures to an unmistakable identification of the Church, at all levels of its life, with those who are victims of oppression (Lichtenberger, 1964).

3

What is impressive is the leaders' full realization of strong member resistance to their racial policies. A document distributed by the national council of the Protestant Episcopal Church in December 1963 explicitly recognized the price of commitment to racial inclusiveness:

> Involvement in the racial crisis is bound to be costly. As Bishop Warnecke pointed out in his report to the House of Bishops, "dioceses and the national Church may shortly have to face greatly reduced giving to the program of the Church because of the position which the Church has taken" (National Council, Protestant Episcopal Church, 1963).

These words were indeed prophetic. In April 1965 St. John's Episcopal Church in Savannah, Georgia, one of the oldest in the nation and the church providing the largest amount of financial support to its diocese, withdrew from the Episcopal Church to become an independent congregation. This action was a specific response to an addition to church law stating that no communicant shall "be excluded from the worship or sacrament of the church . . . because of his race, color, or ethnic origin."[1] In 1970 the Episcopal Church eliminated 43 positions—about 20 percent of its staff at national headquarters. Later that year it decided to cut the remaining national staff by one-half between January 1 and June 30, 1971. Most persons to be dismissed were clergymen and other skilled professionals. The reasons stated for the decline in national giving that necessitated these cuts were "reaction against liberal positions by the major denominations on social issues and a growing belief that mission funds could be more effectively spent at the local rather than regional or national levels" (Fiske, 1970).

The Episcopal Church is but one of several denominations that in the 1960s set racial policies that their leaders believed to be firmly founded on the core values of the church but that they knew would be detrimental to maintenance of the membership and financial strength of their organizations. Although such actions were more dramatic at the national level, local

---

1. St. John's returned to the Episcopal Church in 1969.

church leaders—chiefly ministers but sometimes lay leaders as well—were also striving for such policies. Witness leaders who urged their churches to remain in racially changing neighborhoods and minister to the new residents as well as to the old members. These are startling facts for those scholars who believe, with Michels, that leaders always displace the basic values of their organizations if those values conflict with policies that would maintain the leaders' power.

## Michels's Iron Law of Oligarchy

> It is organization which gives birth to the dominion of the elected over the electors, of the mandataries over the mandators, of the delegates over the delegators. Who says organization, says oligarchy (Michels, 1962:365).

The interesting and complex discussion that leads up to the statement of Michels's self-proclaimed "fundamental sociological law" actually contains two assertions that are not clearly distinguished. The first is that effective organization necessarily involves decision making by a handful of leaders. The treatment of complex issues requires a division of labor in which leaders specialize, gaining an expertise indispensable to the organization but not available to the rank and file (Michels, 1962:124). The experts coordinate the organization's activities; but in addition, because "the problems of the hour often need a speedy decision," leaders are empowered to act without consulting the membership (1962:79).

The second assertion is that control by a handful of leaders inevitably leads to goal displacement; that is, leaders use organizational resources for their own purposes. "By a universally applicable social law, every organ of the collectivity, brought into existence through the need for the division of labor, creates for itself, as soon as it becomes consolidated, interests peculiar to itself. The existence of these special interests involves a necessary conflict with the interests of the collectivity" (Michels,

1962:353). A takeover by leaders pursuing their own goals is simple because most members have too little interest in organizational affairs to pay close attention to them. Even if members watched leaders more carefully, the members' lack of education and decision-making experience would leave them incompetent to judge leaders' actions. On the other hand, leaders gain prestige and power from their positions. Even the leader who takes office reluctantly "will not readily be induced to return to the comparatively obscure position which he formerly occupied" (Michels, 1962:206). Leaders thus ignore the membership's will, neglect the goals for which the organization was formed, and base policy primarily on preservation of the organization and of their power and perquisites within it.[2]

My quarrel is with the second assertion, which has contributed to the neglect of an important sociological phenomenon: the transformation of individuals into collectivities that have lives of their own. Policies at variance with members' desires do not inevitably derive from leaders' vested interests, and majority will is not the only basis for legitimate leadership. Indeed, the primary function of leadership is to create a whole that is not the sum of the parts (LaPiere, 1954:137). Walter Buckley (1967:143) describes "emergent" properties of collectivities "that have no counterpart in corresponding attributes of individuals and that cannot be adequately explained in terms of individual motives."

Ironically, Michels was aware of the emergent character of collectivities and, his genuine alarm notwithstanding, was not opposed to organization. On the contrary, "the realization of a complex of ideal aims [requires] an organization" (1962:61). "Organization appears the only means for the creation of a collective will" (1962:61). "The principle of organization is an absolute essential condition for the political struggle of the masses" (1962:62). Yet, unlike Max Weber, who was also aware of the

2. For extended commentaries on Michels's work see Lipset (1962) and Linz (1968). Empirical works inspired by Michels include Harrison (1959), Lipset, Trow, and Coleman (1962), Wood (1970), and Schmidt (1973).

dangers as well as the values of organization, Michels did not pursue the positive side of organization.

Why did Michels not view the emergent character of organizations—that is, their objective existence as something more than the sum of their individual members—as a positive element of society? From a contemporary perspective, there are at least two reasons. First, he was so preoccupied with the fragility of direct government that he failed to come to grips with the great variations in the ways that different organizations attempt to establish legitimate leadership tactics. From his perspective, there could be only pure democracy or oligarchy. In one sense, of course, this is a truism. If all the people do not govern, then a subset governs. However, Michels believed that leaders would never represent faithfully the basic interests or values of their followers: "for democracy . . . the first appearance of professional leadership marks the beginning of the end" (1962:72). He gave examples of what could conceivably be legitimate leadership decisions yet spoke of a leader as one who has acquired "a freedom of action which he *ought not to* possess" (1962:72, emphasis added). He understood that if leaders did not have this freedom, then "the party becomes incapable of acting in alliance with others, and loses its political elasticity" (1962:79), but he firmly rejected the sincerity of leaders who make decisions unpopular with members.

> This abuse of power may perhaps find justification on tactical grounds, the leaders alleging in defense of their procedure the supreme need that a strike should be declared cautiously and in unison. They claim the right to decide the merits of the question on the sole ground that they know better than the workers themselves the conditions of the labor market throughout the country and are consequently more competent to judge the chances of success in the struggle. The trade-union leaders add that since the stoppage of work in a town necessarily impairs the financial strength of the union in that town, and sometimes disturbs the conditions of work of a whole series of organized workers, it is for the leaders to decide when and where a strike should be declared. Thus they consider that their action is justified by the

democratic aim of safeguarding the interests of the majority
against the impulsive actions of the minority" (1962:160).

Michels uniformly rejected the legitimacy of such actions
by leaders rather than treating legitimacy as a topic for empirical investigation. This unempirical approach caused Alvin
Gouldner (1955:505) to conclude that metaphysical "pathos,"
not "the compulsion of rigorous analysis," led Michels and others to believe that the process of organization would defeat collective ends.

A second explanation of Michels's refusal to view the emergent character of organizations as a positive element in society
may be that he was distracted by certain empirical observations
that were important then but that are no longer valid. Societal
changes since the first publication of *Political Parties* in 1911
have eroded leaders' ability to pursue their vested interests.
First, the wide gap between leaders' and followers' education
and culture has greatly narrowed. The picture now is quite different from that painted by Michels: "In the parties of the pro-
letariat the leaders are, in matters of education, greatly superior
to the led" (1962:107). "Whilst their occupation and the needs
of daily life render it impossible for the masses to attain to a
profound knowledge of the social machinery, and above all of
the working of the political machine, the leader of working-
class origin is enabled, thanks to his new situation, to make
himself intimately familiar with all the technical details of public life and thus to increase his superiority over the rank and
file" (1962:108). Michels recognized that leaders needed considerable education in order to be competent, yet he also believed that education inevitably became a basis for leaders'
power to use the masses to achieve leaders' ends: "When the
workers choose leaders for themselves, they are with their own
hands creating new masters whose principal means of domin-
ion is found in their better instructed minds" (1962:108–109).

Today most people have more education and more leisure
time and other resources for keeping abreast of current issues.
In the United States the rate of illiteracy has decreased from

7.7 percent in 1910 to 1.0 percent in 1970. In 1909 the rate of daily newspaper circulation was 26 per 100 people; in 1973 it was 30 per 100 (U.S. Bureau of the Census). That increase is small, but the effect of newspapers has been enhanced by radio and television. In 1974 there were 1.7 radios per person in the United States, and 0.5 television sets. A recent poll showed that on a typical day almost half of all adult Americans watch a news program on television (A. C. Nielsen Company).

Also, most Americans now enjoy considerably more time for leisure activities than when Michels wrote. Department of Labor statistics show that in the United States in 1910 the average worker spent 52.1 hours on the job each week; by 1970 that figure had decreased to 39.6 hours. In 1909, 92 percent of industrial wage earners worked more than 48 hours a week (Moore and Hedges, 1971); by 1972 the percentage had decreased to 14 (International Labor Office, 1974).

Now that many followers have the ability—that is, the education and time—to watch leaders effectively, the leaders are less likely to abuse power. Furthermore, a complex of technological changes (for example, television) and sociological changes (for example, less automatic respect for authority) has greatly increased the risk that followers will wake from their apathy (Wood, 1970). Even the Teamsters' Union, considered by some to epitomize the abuse of power that Michels saw as inevitable, has a well-organized rebellion growing within its ranks. The group has distributed a 177-page research report to bolster its challenge to the present leadership (Cowan, 1976), and a national television network featured a series of special news reports on the union.

In previous work I have documented both the arousal of church people from apathy toward church policies and the considerable resources that have been marshaled in resistance to denominational policies. Generally, denominational policy makers have exerted more control over policy than anticipated by their denominations' polity. Paul Harrison found "the iron law of oligarchy" an apt description of the development of leader control in the American Baptist Convention. Though of-

ficial theology and polity strongly deny Baptist leaders and
agencies power over constituent congregations, their power is
"oftentimes considerably greater than the official ecclesiastical
authority of the Episcopalian or Methodist bishop, or the Presbyterian moderator" (Harrison, 1959:92). Malcolm Burton's
(1953) polemic against trends toward centralization in the Congregational Christian Churches documents a similar pattern.
My own interviews among Southern Baptists and Disciples led
to the same conclusion: even among the churches with a congregational polity, leaders normally exercise a high degree of
control over policy (Wood, 1967; 1970).

The ferment over civil rights, however, disturbed members'
apathy and changed this situation markedly. Once awakened,
members utilized power resources to influence policy. Tactics of
opposition included letters and resolutions, rejection of denominational literature, withholding of funds, expulsion of liberal ministers, withdrawal of members, decisions by congregations to leave their denominations, and formation of
resistance organizations (Wood and Zald, 1966; Wood, 1967).
Resistance organizations are of special interest here because
their purpose was largely to arouse the rank and file from their
apathy. One resistance group stated its purpose "to oppose, actively and intelligently, the integration of the two races in our
churches and church activities." An unofficial organization was
deemed necessary because the "last three General Conferences
of The Methodist Church" had made it clear that "no official
body of The Methodist Church . . . is free to oppose actively The
Methodist Church on this issue." The group urged laymen to
wake up and take steps against the denomination: "The official
Board of every one of our churches should consult with its assigned minister. At any time that a new minister is assigned, a
new consultation should be had promptly. A policy and a procedure should be agreed upon. A failure to do this will cause
confusion, and could possibly result in your being integrated to
some extent before you even realize it" (see Wood, 1967:139).

The most direct result of resistance was the surrender by denominational officials of much of the unofficial power they had

accrued. This surrender had a profound effect on denominational policy, but the greatest effect was on those officials who after surrender of unofficial power were left with little or no formally legitimated power. In a study of 28 major religious bodies, I demonstrated that denominations with formally legitimate power were more likely than those without it to have strong racial integration policies. This association between policy strength and formal legitimacy persisted even when theology, regional membership, and size were held constant (Wood, 1970).

Whether Michels did not develop his thoughts on the positive aspects of leadership because organizational members of his day seemed incompetent in organizational skills and impervious in their apathy or for some other reason, his argument against organization assumes that majority will is the only allowable basis for legitimacy. This book challenges that assumption.

### Organizational Transcendence and the Problem of Legitimacy

*Organizational transcendence*, a variety of emergence, refers to an organization's use of its name and other resources in actions not predictable from its members' attitudes toward those actions (Wood, 1975). This is a new term, but the basic idea is deeply rooted in the sociological literature.[3] Robert Merton, for example, contrasting the level of motivational analysis with that of institutional or structural analysis, states that "different motivations in a given institutional setting may take approximately the same social expression" (1957:532). Scott Greer's (1955) account of union members' collective support for strikes that they personally oppose exemplifies emergence. As Greer demonstrates, the outcome of a vote cannot be predicted from individual attitudes because social structure mediates between individuals' attitudes (whether they personally want a

---

3. Compare, however, Amitai Etzioni's (1968:32) use of the term *transcendental.*

strike) and their actions (their votes). Other sociological discussions of group behavior transcending the attitudes and desires of individual members include: Nagel (1961:366–397); Blau (1964); Durkheim (1964:10); Etzioni (1968:chap. 3); Wallace (1969); Blau and Schoenherr (1971); Lazarsfeld et al. (1972:228); and Turner and Killian (1972:21–25).

Thus, when appropriate mechanisms of social control are effective, organizations' policies and actions may differ from the average of their members' personal views. Furthermore, such transcendence can exist even when the opposed members are fully aware of the policies. As a broad term, *transcendence* includes oligarchy. The advantage of the term is that it allows us to think of both legitimate and illegitimate transcendence. Michels considered only illegitimate transcendence—oligarchy, which he believed to be inevitable.

This book focuses on how formal legitimacy and belief in legitimacy facilitate transcendence. For example, members may allow transcendence because they understand that the act of joining a particular polity binds them to abide by decisions consistent with that polity; that is, the decisions are formally legitimate. Thus, when convinced that due process has been followed, they generally will support leaders' actions even when they dislike them. Another source of transcendence is members' belief in leaders' legitimacy, regardless of whether that legitimacy has been institutionalized in the organization's polity. We shall see that there are several possible bases for such belief.

The concept of legitimacy is based on the concept of law in its broad sense of rule based on authority or custom, or, more broadly, rooted in society. Legitimacy, then, implies an established standard of behavior for leader actions. Legitimacy also can be a lever that leaders use to secure their actions: leaders claim legitimacy so that *organizational* actions can occur. Granted that organizations transcend individuals, majority will clearly is not always an appropriate basis for legitimacy. However, to establish a basis for legitimacy that allows collective action but does not do violence to the norms of a democratic society may appear to be impossible.

Arthur Stinchcombe (1968) emphasized the more objective aspect of legitimacy, which creates a readiness on the part of other centers of power to back up a legitimate authority, for example, with police power. He did not entirely discount the importance of subordinates' perceptions of legitimacy, but he held that "power based only on the shifting sands of public opinion and willing obedience is inherently unstable" (1968:161). In contrast, Weber (1968) implied that every form of domination—in a sense, any transcendence involves domination of individuals by a collectivity—attempts to establish belief in its legitimacy. That is, leaders try to ensure that their directives and other actions are perceived as legitimate by members.[4] Any one of a number of motives, from "simple habituation to the most rational calculations of advantage," may influence people voluntarily to allow themselves to be dominated by a social order. However, because these motives do not form a "sufficiently reliable basis for a given domination," a "system attempts to establish and cultivate a belief in legitimacy" (1968:213).

In his discussion of the bases on which leaders might claim legitimacy, Weber described his famous pure types of authority (1968:215). *Legal authority* makes a claim to legitimacy that is based on rational grounds; *traditional authority* rests on "an established belief in the sanctity of immemorial tradition and the legitimacy of those exercising authority under them"; *charismatic authority* relies on "devotion to the exceptional sanctity, heroism, or exemplary character of an individual person and of the normative patterns for order revealed or ordained by him." Tradition is still important in contemporary organizations, and charismatic leadership is certainly not unknown, but legal authority, especially that derived from a voluntary agreement between interested parties, is most often stressed. Today, however, with the prevalence of democratic norms, the general ero-

4. Weber (1968) confined his discussion to specific commands. I have generalized his logic.

sion of authority, the tendency toward membership in more
than one organization, and the increased movement of individuals from organization to organization, leadership is ever more
difficult to maintain purely on the basis of belief in the legality
of leaders' actions.

This book assesses whether formal legitimacy can elicit
members' support for unpopular policies and whether a belief
in legitimacy is needed to reinforce formal legitimacy. Drawing
on Weber and others, I develop a concept of legitimacy that is
grounded in the collective values fostered by an organization. I
argue that, at least in voluntary organizations, leadership that
bases its claim to legitimacy on the collective values of the organization will be more effective than that based on rational-legal
claims. Indeed, in a democratic society this type of legitimacy
seems essential when the core values of an organization lead to
policies disliked by the majority of its members.

## Organization of This Study

The thesis of this book is that policies out of line with
members' desires may result from leaders' attempts to carry out
their responsibility to direct the group in the implementation of
its values; that is, such policies do not necessarily constitute
goal displacement. In addition, I argue that leaders are most
effective, at least in areas of controversy, when they claim legitimacy on the basis of the organization's values. The two central
questions are: Why do members oppose policies that derive
from the core values of their organizations? What is legitimacy's
role in inducing members to support unpopular policies?

A preliminary answer to the first question is that members of
a particular organization also belong to other networks of social
interaction.[5] In each social network they learn values and are
subject to varying degrees of social control. Thus, members
may find themselves opposed to the policies of a particular or-

5. I use the phrase "networks of social interaction" rather than the term *subcultures* because it is broad enough to include both subcultures and less stable,
less intense networks that also teach and reinforce values.

ganization because they have been socialized to contrary values elsewhere and, for the moment, feel the balance of their ties pulling them in another direction (Coleman, 1957). In this case it is not theoretically appropriate, though it may be practically so, for leaders simply to poll members to determine organizational action; the majority might favor actions that would betray the organization's core values, which the leaders have been mandated to foster. Two illustrations will emphasize how values promoted in one network of social interaction may cause individuals to disapprove of the behavior fostered by another network, *even though the second is legitimately pursuing its core values.* First, imagine a Methodist member of the Ku Klux Klan. As a member of the Klan he would disapprove of The United Methodist Church's stand on racial equality. Nonetheless, the church should discount this member's disapproval because it derives from the opposing values of another organization. In the second illustration, the Catholic Church in the South refused to yield to the dramatic protest of Catholic lay people against integration of parochial schools in the 1950s and 1960s. The church leaders rightly saw that protesters were acting out values derived from sources other than the church.

This book explores how membership in various networks of social interaction affects members' opposition to their local church's implementation of its core values. Specifically, I suggest that ministers' social networks reinforce their allegiance to the church's core values while members' networks tend to reinforce contrary values.

The question of legitimacy's role in gaining support is addressed in a search for the conditions that enable leaders to enlist members' support for policies they oppose. This study looks at two types of conditions: structural and ideological. Structural conditions include the legitimacy of leadership built into the formal structure of the organization (formal legitimacy), financial solvency, and the size of the organization. Ideological conditions include members' belief in the legitimacy of organizational leaders, leaders' belief in the legitimacy of the national organization, and members' tolerance of policies that they dislike. Knowledge of the conditions that lead to organizational transcendence is a basis for evaluating Michels's assertion that goal displacement is inevitable.

Data for the study were gathered in Indianapolis, Indiana, during the fall of 1973 and the spring of 1974. A comparison with other Standard Metropolitan Statistical Areas (SMSAs) reveals that Indianapolis is in most respects typical of urban America (Knoke and Wood, 1981). Indianapolis was near the mean on 14 of 15 indicators of population composition, type of employment, income, and education. (The atypical feature of Indianapolis was its much smaller percentage of foreign-born residents.)

By 1973 the high tide of sentiment in favor of civil rights that resulted in the Civil Rights Acts of 1964 and 1965 had long since subsided. The severe storm of reaction to the churches' role in the movements of the 1960s had also calmed somewhat, but it appeared that members would never again be apathetic about their local churches' social actions. Nineteen seventy-three was a good time for the questions: Could local church leaders involve their churches in social actions that the majority of their members opposed? Was it legitimate for them to do so?

Data for this study consist of questionnaires answered by 2,165 members of 58 local churches in Indianapolis, questionnaires answered by 204 of their officers, and both questionnaires and interview schedules answered by each of their 58 ministers. Budgets, reports, and other documents of the churches were also analyzed.

The initial step in choosing the sample was a purposive selection of mainline Protestant denominations. (One operational definition of a mainline denomination is a denomination with more than one million members nationally.) These denominations are important because their actions have a detectable impact on American society. Further, it was theoretically important to restrict the analysis to liberal denominations, that is, those that had taken controversial stands and become involved enough in social action to have experienced considerable resistance from their members. I wanted denominations whose members were most likely to have been aroused from their apathy toward church policy. I identified seven such denominations: The United Methodist Church, The United Presbyterian Church in the United States of America, The Episcopal Church, the Lutheran Church in America, the Christian Church (Disciples of Christ), the American Baptist Churches in the U.S.A., and the United Church of Christ.[6]

Having chosen these denominations to suit my theoretical purposes, I then drew a sample of their local churches in Indianapolis, with the probability of a church being chosen proportional to its size. My specific interest in how church leaders gained their churches' support for racial justice policies led to the exclusion of those few churches that traditionally had a totally black membership. From the membership rolls of each church chosen I then drew a random sample of members. The result was a sample that allowed me to analyze data at two levels. I have a sample of 58 local churches—the organizational units of analysis—that are representative of liberal, mainline Protestant churches in Indianapolis. I also have a sample of church people who, after weighting to minimize the overrepresentation of females and frequent church attenders among respondents, are representative of members of mainline Protestant church members in Indianapolis. Complete sampling details appear in Appendix A.

Chapters 2 and 3 analyze the sample of church members using individual members as units of analysis. Chapter 2 establishes that many members have attitudes contrary to the core values of their church, especially in the areas of racial and economic justice. The chapter describes sharp differences between members' and leaders' attitudes toward the church's advocacy of certain challenged values of our society and then asks why these differences have caused so little conflict. Chapter 3 describes the sources of these differences, focusing on differences between members' and ministers' networks of social interaction

6. These are the official names of the denominations as listed in the *Yearbook of American and Canadian Churches, 1980*, ed. Constant H. Jacquet, Jr. (Nashville, Tenn.: Abingdon, 1980).

and especially on the differential impact of organizations outside the church.

In the fourth and subsequent chapters local churches rather
than members are the units of analysis. Chapter 4 describes
local churches' social action and relates it to the churches' various characteristics, including members' and ministers' attitudes.
Chapter 5 treats the conditions that enable some churches to
transcend members' opposition to social action and the legitimacy of such transcendence. The final chapter uses this study
of churches as a basis for reflection on a more general theory of
leadership in voluntary organizations and on the implications of
the theory for Michels's iron law of oligarchy.

2

---

# Dissension between Local Church Members and Their Leaders

Dissension between church members and their leaders has attracted widespread scholarly and popular interest since the mid-1950s. Of course, the specific issues in contention concern other voluntary organizations as well as the churches. This dissension is of particular importance to the present study, however, because an empirical critique of Michels's iron law of oligarchy requires a situation in which organizational leaders desire policies at variance with members' desires. Where there is no disagreement, the question of the legitimacy of the leadership is less pressing.

This chapter will assess church members' and leaders' (ministers' and lay leaders') willingness for the church to address secular issues and describe the attitudes toward three issues that are closely related to core values of the church: equality of economic opportunity; racial equality; and the position of women in society. Finally, I shall examine why sharp differences between members and ministers have not resulted in more conflict. My purpose is to prepare for later discussion of the social sources of these attitudes and of leaders' resources for implementing organizational values that are challenged by the attitudes that members assimilate from the surrounding society.

## The Church and Social Issues

Church members are sometimes pictured as not wanting the church to deal in any way with the outside world or as wanting complete accommodation to the established powers outside the church (Niebuhr, 1951). As a whole, my sample of mainline Protestants falls between these two extremes. Most laymen see social action as relevant to the church, but most do not want their church to make social and political questions a primary focus of its ministry. Two-thirds of the members believed that "the local church should concern itself with the problems and needs of its members rather than with social and political problems." Nevertheless, 62 percent disagreed with the statement that their denomination should "stick to religion," and 69 percent disagreed that their ministers should do so.

On specific issues an even greater percentage of members were willing for the church to be socially involved, but they were concerned about which side of an issue the church would support. For example, only 10 percent would approve their local church taking a stand *for* busing of schoolchildren to achieve racial balance in the school system, but 62 percent would approve a stand *against* busing. Thus, 72 percent are willing for the church to be involved in this controversial secular issue. Furthermore, 69 percent would be willing for their church to have a birth control clinic, 76 percent would be willing for their church to house a Headstart program, and 79 percent would approve its joining with other organizations in legal action against a factory that was polluting its community. At the very most, only 21 percent of these church members want the church to concern itself solely with religion in the narrower sense of that word. On the basis of H. Richard Niebuhr's work, one might expect a somewhat worldly orientation among these church people (these churches are far closer to "church" than to "sect"), but the support for actions that challenge the status quo is surprising.

Evidence also suggests that church people are as willing to see their church engage in social action as they are to see their secular organizations do so. Church members who belonged to at least one organization outside the church—about three-fourths of the sample—were asked several questions about the nonchurch organization most important to them personally.

When asked whether it is right for the organization to take actions on political and social issues, 38 percent answered "yes" and another 21 percent answered "sometimes." The combined figure is slightly less than the 63 percent who felt the church should not concern itself solely with religion.

Most church members were willing for their churches to be involved in controversy; only 35 percent agreed with the statement that "a local church should never engage in any activities which would cause important people in the community to respect its members less." The solidary character of the church had led me to expect that most church members would place a high value on keeping peace within the congregation, but I was wrong. Almost two-thirds of the respondents were willing for the church to engage in issues that divide members, and 64 percent disagreed that "a *local church* should not engage in any activities which might cause it to lose members."

Though church people were willing for the church to act on secular issues, they nonetheless had reservations about actions that might provoke violence. For example, 69 percent were willing for ministers to become involved in social action, but only 48 percent were willing to have their minister involved in a picket line or demonstration.

Marvin Olsen's protest actions legitimacy scale (see Olsen and Baden, 1974) revealed a similar concern for order. When asked what actions dissatisfied groups have a right to take in order to express their dissatisfaction, church members approved the listed alternatives by the following percentages: boycott or petition, 89 percent; public speeches and rallies, 86 percent; march quietly and peacefully, 72 percent; mass demonstrations with large crowds, 36 percent; sit-ins or walk-outs, 29 percent; break laws, 4 percent.

Overall, the data indicated that most church members were not opposed to social action by their church, even when it challenged the status quo, so long as they agreed with the church's stand on the issue and believed that order would be maintained. Douglas Johnson and George Cornell (1972) went too far in reassuring leaders of the denominations they studied that the ma-

jority support social action. My findings suggest that much of
the social action of several of their denominations is of the
order-challenging kind. And, as we shall see, there is far less
support for the church's social action ministry among lay members than among ministers, and members' positions on the issues are more conservative than those of ministers.

## Members' and Leaders' Attitudes Compared

Michels was convinced that leaders are almost always
more conservative than members. In contrast, Samuel Stouffer
reported in *Communism, Conformity, and Civil Liberties* (1963)
that organizational leaders are more liberal than followers on
civil liberties issues. He explained that the leaders are more
likely to have had to make decisions about these issues or to
have imagined that they would be faced by them (1963:48).
Also, as community leaders they are "especially responsible and
thoughtful citizens, [and] are more likely than the rank and file
to give a sober second thought to the dangers involved in deny-
ing civil liberties to those whose views they dislike" (1963:27).
Apparently, then, leaders feel compelled to guide organizational
behavior by the universal values that their organizations usually espouse rather than by the more particular values that
often produce individuals' first response to issues. This commitment to values is, I believe, one of the foundations of legitimate
leadership.

Table 2.1 compares the attitudes of lay members, lay officers,
and ministers toward aspects of the question we have been discussing. The ministers and members differ sharply; lay officers
fall between the other two groups, but nearer to the rank and
file than to the clergy.

We turn now to the specific issues that are the focus of
the present study. The most talked about social issues in the
churches at the time of this study were those of economic opportunity, racial equality, and the changing rights and roles of
women.

Table 2.1. Comparison of Attitudes toward Social Action by Churches

| Questionnaire items | Members | Lay officers | Ministers |
|---|---|---|---|
| | *Percentage disagreeing* | | |
| "My denomination should stick to religion and not concern itself with social and political problems." | 62 | 70 | 98 |
| "Ministers should stick to religion and not concern themselves with social, economic, and political questions." | 68 | [a] | 94 |
| | *Percentage agreeing* | | |
| "I would support my minister if he were to participate in a picket line or demonstration on behalf of underprivileged people."[b] | 48 | 52 | 80 |
| "My denomination should use its resources to fight social injustice." | 60 | 68 | 96 |
| I would approve if my local church "publicly *opposed* busing of school children for the purpose of achieving a racial balance in Indianapolis schools." | 62 | 51 | 32 |
| "Churches should refuse to do business with firms unwilling to hire blacks on the same basis as whites." | 45 | 52 | 74 |
| I would approve if my local church "let a birth control clinic use church facilities." | 69 | 69 | 91 |

Table 2.1, *continued.*

| Questionnaire items | Members | Lay officers | Ministers |
|---|---|---|---|
| I would approve if my local church "publicly endorsed equal rights for women." | 70 | 76 | 87 |
| I would approve if my local church "let a Headstart program use church facilities five days a week." | 76 | *a* | 95 |

[a]This question was not included in the questionnaire for lay officers.
[b]The ministers' form of this question began "It is proper for a minister to. . . ."

EQUALITY OF ECONOMIC OPPORTUNITY

In contrast to their ministers, mainline Protestants have a rather conservative view of economic opportunity in America. They believe that the sources of poverty are individualistic rather than structural, as reflected in the agreement of 82 percent of the respondents that "In American society, any individual with ability and ambition can earn a good income." Respondents also rated eleven sources of poverty as very important, important, or not important. I then ranked the sources according to the percentage of respondents who rated them very important. Table 2.2 lists the ranks and the percentages, together with those of a sample of the national population reported by Joe Feagin (1975), who devised this means of assessing attitudes toward poverty.

Two of the four causes assigned highest importance by members (lack of effort, lack of thrift) place blame on the individual for his or her poverty. The other two (sickness and lack of ability) blame neither the individual nor society but something (fate) beyond the control of either. Structural explanations are at the bottom of the list. It is logical to expect, then, that mainline Protestants would not appreciate attempts by their churches to change the structure of American society.

One item on the questionnaire stated specifically, "The church should direct some of its activities toward changing the structure of American society." Although 63 percent agreed with that statement, only 32 percent agreed that "Denominations should use their corporate power to change the structure of our society." This finding is congruent with Mary Taylor's (1975) conclusion that one California presbytery's use of corporate power and its dedication to structural change discouraged lay participation in social action and widened the gulf between clergy and laity.

The ministers' responses were much different. Whereas 82 percent of the members agreed that "In American society, any individual with ability and ambition can earn a good income," only 31 percent of the ministers agreed. The contrast on explanations for poverty is equally dramatic (Table 2.2). According to the ministers, the most important explanations are prejudice and discrimination, low wages in some businesses and industries, and the failure of society to provide good schools. All three are structural explanations, and all were given low rankings by the members. Clearly, ministers should be more appreciative of church action to change the structure of society. Ninety percent of the ministers, compared with 61 percent of the lay members, thought that "The church should direct some of its activities toward changing the structure of American society." Though only 32 percent of the members thought that denominations should use their corporate power to change the structure of our society, 71 percent of the ministers thought so.

RACIAL EQUALITY

Members and ministers also disagreed on racial equality. Most members sympathized with the plight of blacks, but sympathy among ministers was almost universal. Fifty-four percent of the members believed they could "understand why black people are sometimes driven to violence," but 91 percent of the ministers held that belief. A gap of similar magnitude divided lay people and ministers in their responses to two items that relate church response to the racial issue. About half (52 per-

Table 2.2. Members' and Ministers' Views of the Sources of Poverty

| Sources of poverty listed in questionnaire (I = individualistic; F = fate; S = structural) | Indianapolis members | | National sample | | Indianapolis ministers | |
|---|---|---|---|---|---|---|
| | Percentage responding "very important" | (Rank) | Percentage responding "very important" | (Rank) | Percentage responding "very important" | (Rank) |
| Lack of effort by the poor themselves. (I) | 46 | (1) | 55 | (2) | 14 | (10) |
| Sickness and physical handicaps. (F) | 45 | (2) | 46 | (5) | 35 | (5) |
| Lack of thrift and proper money management by poor people. (I) | 45 | (3) | 58 | (1) | 31 | (6; tie) |
| Lack of ability and talent among poor people. (F) | 44 | (4) | 52 | (3) | 25 | (8) |
| Failure of society to provide good schools for many Americans. (S) | 41 | (5) | 36 | (7) | 52 | (3) |
| Loose morals and drunkenness. (I) | 38 | (6) | 48 | (4) | 12 | (11) |
| Low wages in some businesses and industries. (S) | 37 | (7) | 42 | (6) | 60 | (2) |
| Prejudice and discrimination against blacks. (S) | 28 | (8) | 33 | (8) | 68 | (1) |
| Failure of private industry to provide enough jobs. (S) | 21 | (9) | 27 | (9) | 20 | (9) |
| Being taken advantage of by rich people. (S) | 20 | (10) | 18 | (10) | 31 | (6; tie) |
| Just bad luck. (F) | 8 | (11) | 8 | (11) | 36 | (4) |

cent) of the members, but less than a fourth (23 percent) of the ministers, would oppose their church's holding "a marriage ceremony for an interracial couple." And less than half (45 percent) of the members, but three-fourths (74 percent) of the ministers, believed that "Churches should refuse to do business with firms unwilling to hire blacks on the same basis as whites."

Finally, an item that mixed both economic opportunity and racial equality drew the lowest degree of agreement, but the gap between members and ministers remained. Nineteen percent of the members and 47 percent of the ministers thought that "American churches should provide money for the economic advancement of black Americans."

RIGHTS AND ROLES OF WOMEN

The attitudes of mainline Protestants appeared to be quite liberal on the issue of changing rights and roles of women, but those of their ministers were, for the most part, even more liberal. Eighty percent of the members and 98 percent (all but one) of the ministers disagreed with the statement that "Women, if they work at all, should take feminine positions such as nursing, secretarial work, or child care." Nor do church people support economic discrimination against women. Eighty-six percent of the members and 98 percent of the ministers disagreed with the statement that "There is nothing wrong in paying women less than men for doing similar work when they are not the major 'breadwinners' in the family." Furthermore, church people see nothing wrong in women's engaging in politics: 92 percent of the members and 98 percent of the ministers disagreed that "Women should stay out of politics." Although fewer respondents believed that the church should publicly endorse equal rights for women, support was nevertheless strong: 70 percent of the members and 91 percent of the ministers approved of such an endorsement. Finally, 62 percent of the sample would approve if their local church "secured a woman as senior minister."

## Why Differences Lead to Relatively Little Conflict

The overall picture that emerges from a comparison of members' and ministers' attitudes on the three social issues is one of a gap between ministers' and lay people's attitudes. In the case of changing rights and roles of women, this gap does not appear likely to cause dissension. Lay people's attitudes have become quite liberal in relation to the traditional views on this subject. The small gap is owing solely to the ministers' even more liberal attitudes. However, on equality of economic opportunity and racial equality the views of the average member and those of the average minister differ substantially. Both the size of the gap and the divergence of ideas about appropriate strategies suggest a real possibility of dissension—precisely the phenomenon presented by Jeffrey Hadden in *The Gathering Storm in the Churches* (1969).

Hadden's incisive book not only documented the gap between the views of ministers and church members vis-à-vis social issues but also confronted its implications. One of Hadden's major questions was: Given the sometimes extreme differences between members and ministers, why has there not been even more conflict over social issues within the church? Hadden's primary answer was that the ministers with more liberal views on social action were structurally insulated from members, occupying positions in the denominational bureaucracy or in the campus ministry. Although this insulation allowed the ministers to continue to take controversial positions despite strong opposing voices, it also led to the intense polarization that Hadden called "the gathering storm."

Hadden argues convincingly and documents his explanation well. Yet it is important to note that different types of denominational structure provide differential insulation for leaders who espouse controversial views. My 1972 comparative study of editors of Sunday school literature shows that editors in a congregational denomination (the Southern Baptist Convention) were necessarily far more sensitive to lay pressure than were editors in a hierarchical one (The Methodist Church). A brief review of that study will illustrate a central theme of this book: how formal polity affects the formation and implementation of controversial policy.

In 1967 Southern Baptist literature was almost wholly lacking in treatment of integration, with the exception of general statements about Christian brotherhood. On the other hand, Methodist literature endorsed such civil rights leaders as Martin Luther King, Jr., and was filled with pictures showing blacks and whites together.[1] Yet among Baptist staff members, as well as among the Methodists, I found many who expressed a deep personal conviction that the church should be actively involved in securing civil rights for blacks. The difference appeared to be the restraints placed upon Baptist editors by their editor-in-chief, restraints that derived, in turn, from those placed on the editor-in-chief by the Southern Baptist constituency.

Because of its congregational polity, the Southern Baptist Convention must be sensitive to the will of its churches. This point is illustrated by the addition made to the statement that the Convention finally adopted on civil rights: "This convention of Baptists recognizes the authority and competency of every local church affiliated with the Southern Baptist Convention in dealing with any question, social or otherwise" (Burton, 1965).

The Baptist editor-in-chief was extremely sensitive to the mood of the Convention because "the Convention could close down the Sunday School Board if it so desired."[2] The insecure

1. Comparison of the two denominational agencies is based on interviews with agency personnel, examination of organizational communications (such as memos from editors-in-chief and responses by editors to letters of protest from users of the Sunday school materials), and a review of a sample of the materials produced by the agencies. These data were gathered in 1966 and 1967.

I do not mean to pass judgment on the Southern Baptists. Given their congregational polity and large Southern membership, even these general statements may have been organizationally courageous.

2. This explanation was offered by a high-level staff member in a personal interview.

relationship of the board to the Convention is reflected in a resolution adopted by the 1965 Convention:

> WHEREAS, concern has been expressed to this Convention regarding certain publications of the Sunday School Board, and
> WHEREAS, a desire has been expressed that careful attention be given by the Sunday School Board to the qualifications of persons it engages as writers and speakers, and
> WHEREAS, the Sunday School Board has acknowledged mistakes and has taken steps to prevent their recurrence,
> THEREFORE, BE IT RESOLVED that the Southern Baptist Convention express to the Sunday School Board its appreciation for responsibilities faithfully discharged, and its confidence that diligence will continue to be exercised in all of its activities (Burton, 1965).

The Baptist editor-in-chief was thus constrained to keep close watch over all literature produced by his agency. He apparently had no leverage to defend editors who might get into trouble on the race issue. For example, a furor of protest arose over the inclusion of a book by James Baldwin in a list of supplementary readings for youth. The persons involved found their jobs endangered and were required to make formal apologies.

Note, however, that the Southern Baptist editor-in-chief was sensitive to liberal as well as to conservative moods of the Convention. A slight loosening of control over editors was evident after the 1965 Convention's outspoken stand (relative to previous years) on civil rights. He was noticeably relieved and even ready to "rattle his sabers" a little.[3] This fact substantiates my view that the contrast described here derives more from structural constraints than from individual differences.

An interview with the editor-in-chief of the Methodist board bolstered this view. He stressed his mandate and his intention to carry out the will of the General Conference. When segregationists complained, he relied on the strength of the Methodist structure, quoting them the *Discipline* and the resolutions of the General Conference. Moreover, ample evidence indicated

3. This mood was reported in an interview with the staff member mentioned in note 2.

that the Methodist chief insulated his editors from outside pressures. In fact, he spent much of his time trouble-shooting. A May 1961 bulletin of the Methodist Layman's Union indicated the position the editor-in-chief took on one trouble-shooting trip:

> At our invitation Dr. _____, Editor of Church School Publications of the Methodist Publishing House, Nashville, Tennessee, visited our Committee studying this question in Birmingham December 1959. He then stated categorically that the Methodist Publishing House could not desist from publishing articles persuasive of integrating the Church; that he could not even agree to give our side of the question equal space, or in fact, any space at all. He assigned as his reason for these decisions the fact that previous General Conferences of the Church had spoken, and he was carrying out the mandate of the Church in this regard. He gave us no comfort whatever.[4]

This comparison of Methodist and Southern Baptist literature agencies leads to several conclusions. The hierarchical structure of The Methodist Church placed its publication agency in a more stable relationship to its parent organization. The more secure position allowed the Methodist editor-in-chief to grant his editors more freedom to embody in their work the imperatives of the civil rights movement that were matters of personal concern. Because Methodist literature has a large circulation in the South, however, a great deal of the Methodist chief's time and energy was devoted to defending his editors against resistance forces. In contrast, the Southern Baptist structure dictated extreme caution, and the editor-in-chief was highly sensitive to the constraints imposed by his constituency. The kinds of constraints that he in turn placed upon his editors inhibited their personal desires to champion racial equality.

At the denominational level, Hadden's question about the dampening of conflict is somewhat less pressing at the present time. Despite structural insulation, the prediction implicit in

---

4. Printed letter of the Methodist Layman's Union, May 5, 1961. This organization was formed to counter integration influences in the denomination. For an account of its activities, see Wood and Zald (1966).

the title of Hadden's book came true. As my earlier review of the Episcopal Church shows (see Chapter 1), the storm broke even in the strongest polities. To be sure, the storm of conservative resistance usually did not reverse policy, but it reduced the number of positions in denominational bureaucracies within which liberal ministers could find a haven. Furthermore, any restructuring that resulted from the dissension gave lay members more control over social policy. An example is in the United Presbyterian Church, where a revenue-sharing policy was developed so that most funding of social action was done at the local or regional level.

## Lack of Conflict in the Local Church

In explaining why sharp differences did not lead to even more conflict between church members and ministers, Hadden failed to treat adequately the parish clergy. Sharp differences between ministers and members still exist *in the local parish*, where, though strong polities may provide the minister structural support for social action, no polity can shield the minister from the view of his or her lay people (Quinley, 1974a). Hadden's question certainly remains appropriate at the local church level: Why are local churches not riddled with conflict over social action?

I approached this question with some initial hypotheses. In my earlier study (1967) of lay resistance to social action, I found that conservative members and sometimes whole congregations changed denominations to find more compatible social action views. Shifting within denominations also occurred as particular churches and ministers became known as conservative or, occasionally, as liberal. Generalizing from that study to the present one, it seemed possible that members and ministers might have sorted themselves out so that conservative members were in churches with conservative ministers and liberal members in churches with liberal ministers. Thus, the overall gap between all members and ministers might be extensive, but the gap between the members and minister of a given congregation might be much narrower.

*Hypothesis 2.1.* The gap between the social action views of the members and the minister of any particular church will be narrower than the overall gap between all members and ministers.

Because the role of minister has a great deal of prestige among church people, there may be a tendency for members to misperceive their minister's social action views as compatible with their own (Heider, 1946).

*Hypothesis 2.2.* The actual gap between the social action views of members and their minister will be wider than the gap perceived by members.

Despite sharp differences about social action, ministers and members might have similar views about the areas of ministry in which they interact most often. Thus ministers who did a good job of pastoral counseling and visiting, for example, would have a great resource to draw on in gaining support, or at least tolerance, for their social action views and programs.

*Hypothesis 2.3.* Members and their ministers are in basic agreement about the major responsibilities of the minister.

ATTITUDES

To test the first hypothesis, I devised two attitude scales that were administered to both ministers and members. As these largely middle-class members' attitudes about the changing rights and roles of women were relatively liberal, I focused my attention on the more controversial issues of welfare and racial justice. An example of the items on the welfare scale is: How would you respond if your local church or its leaders "contributed funds to a welfare rights organization"? The racial justice scale included the item: How would you respond if your local church or its leaders "provided space in the church for meetings of the local chapter of the National Association for the Advancement of Colored People"? Complete details of these scales are presented in Appendix A.

On the 20-point welfare scale the average scores were 10.70 for members and 13.55 for ministers, resulting in an overall gap of 2.85 between members and ministers. On the 28-point racial justice scale the overall gap was 2.57, with an average score of 13.41 for members and 15.98 for ministers. I then calculated the difference between a minister's score and the mean score of the members of his congregation. On welfare, 26 churches (45 percent) showed less than the overall gap. The figures for racial justice were similar: 31 churches (53 percent) revealed less than the overall gap.

Another method of assessing the match between members and ministers considered a congregation liberal if its average was above that for all congregations and conservative if below. Similarly, a minister was considered liberal if he scored above the average for all ministers and conservative if he scored below that average. On each scale about two-thirds of the churches whose members' attitudes were below the mean for all members also had ministers whose attitudes were below the mean for all ministers. On the racial justice scale two-thirds of the churches whose members' attitudes were above the mean also had ministers with attitudes above the mean. Thus, in all, 66 percent of the churches could be considered matched on racial justice attitudes using this crude measure. The percentage was lower on the welfare scale. Forty-six percent of the churches whose members' attitudes were above the mean also had ministers with attitudes above the mean. Thus, in all, 57 percent of the churches could be considered matched with their ministers on attitudes toward welfare. On both scales, however, several churches were badly mismatched. In 8 churches on the racial justice scale and 9 on welfare, there existed a gap of more than one standard deviation above the mean. Surprisingly, 10 percent of the churches on each scale had a gap of more than one standard deviation *below* the mean; that is, the members had attitudes appreciably more liberal than those of their ministers.

In summary, the attitudes of members and ministers in most churches differ, and the ministers' attitudes are usually more liberal. Moreover, extreme differences mark about one-fourth of the churches. Though the sorting process lessens the potential for conflict over social action, a high potential for conflict remains in an appreciable number of churches.

MISPERCEPTIONS

With regard to my second hypothesis, some discrepancy appeared between members' perceptions of ministers' attitudes and the actual attitudes. For example, in 7 churches where the majority of members believed the minister held the same views as the congregation, there was in fact a gap of more than one standard deviation above the mean. Conversely, in 12 churches where the members felt the minister did not hold the same views, the gap fell within one standard deviation of the mean. Thus, at least some misperception existed in 33 percent of the churches.

The most striking finding, however, was the lack of relationship between a congregation's perception of the minister's views about social action and its satisfaction with the minister. In the 14 churches in which the majority of members felt the minister did not hold the same views as the congregation, a majority was nevertheless satisfied with the minister, and the average rate of satisfaction, 74 percent, was only 7 percent below the average for the total sample (see Table 2.3). Moreover, the church with the fewest members who believed that the minister held the same views as the congregation had the highest rate of satisfaction (93.9 percent) with the minister.

AGREEMENT ON MINISTERIAL RESPONSIBILITIES

As the data on satisfaction imply, the third hypothesis also received some support from the data. The gap between minis-

Table 2.3. Members' Perception of Their Minister's Views and
Their Satisfaction with the Minister

| Church | Percentage of members who believed their minister held views different from their own | Percentage of members satisfied with their minister |
|---|---|---|
| 1 | 71.9 | 93.9 |
| 2 | 59.5 | 88.0 |
| 3 | 58.8 | 65.2 |
| 4 | 57.9 | 83.4 |
| 5 | 57.8 | 88.8 |
| 6 | 57.3 | 78.6 |
| 7 | 55.3 | 50.5 |
| 8 | 54.8 | 73.2 |
| 9 | 53.8 | 80.0 |
| 10 | 53.4 | 54.8 |
| 11 | 53.0 | 76.3 |
| 12 | 52.4 | 90.0 |
| 13 | 52.0 | 51.8 |
| 14 | 50.9 | 69.1 |

ters' and members' views does not cause conflict even when
members perceive such a gap, in part because most efforts of
ministers are not in the social action area but in more traditional areas where ministers and members are largely in agreement. In comparing members' and ministers' choices of the one
ministerial activity they consider most important, it is apparent
that members and ministers agree on the basic responsibilities
of the minister. In 71 percent of the churches the activity
chosen by the minister (from a list of 13 possibilities) placed at
least third when members' choices were tallied. It should not be
assumed, however, that the rest of the churches were prone to
great controversy. As a matter of fact, the activities that some
ministers chose as most important but that failed to place at
least third among their congregations were: administration
(chosen by 3 ministers); preaching (3); evangelism (1); teaching (1); worship (1); social issues (1). Only 1 percent of the

members and 2 percent of the ministers felt that social issues
were the most important ministerial responsibility.

ADDITIONAL EXPLANATIONS

Each of the hypotheses about the dampened conflict received some support, but they still left much about the lack of
intense local church conflict to be explained. Three additional
elements of an explanation emerged from the research.

One reason members can tolerate ministers' liberal ideas is
that members believe that lay officers have the most influence
on social policies. In the total sample, 52 percent felt that the
official board had the most influence, while only 24 percent felt
that the minister had the most. In 8 of the 14 churches in
which members perceived a gap between themselves and the
minister, the majority of members believed that the official
board had the most influence on decisions about social policies.
In all but one of the churches the majority believed that either
the official board or the members at large had the most influence. In short, most members in each church believed that lay
people had more influence on social policy than the minister
did.

It also appears that certain norms give the minister license to
deviate from members. For example, 65 percent of the members
said that they wanted their minister to feel free to preach a sermon on any social or political issue about which he felt strongly.
Also, in 60 percent of the churches most officers wanted their
minister to have this freedom. These norms could be compared
with those of academic freedom within the university community. In the church the norms of ministerial freedom are anchored in the rich tradition of the Hebrew prophets. As we shall
see in Chapter 6, ministers pursuing controversial policies do
well to prepare the way by evoking prophetic norms.

Ministers' tendency to carry out their social action ministries
in a nonthreatening way also dampens conflict. Overwhelm-
ingly, ministers viewed their role in social action as low-key and
primarily educational. For example, in answering the question,

"How do you perceive *your* role in formulating social policy?"
the 14 ministers whose members' views are reported in Table
2.3 typically responded:

> "The minister is essentially a preaching layman whose role is to
> equip the congregation for responsible decision making."

> "Educating and involving people so that they can see the needs."

> "I'm not authoritarian, don't have all answers, don't want to ap-
> pear to. I want to learn with others. Try to work through key
> people."

> "More indirect than ever before. Minister must deal with people
> where they are and has to raise consciousness. In previous par-
> ishes my involvement has been direct and heavy. But here, that
> just isn't possible."

> "Bringing needs and reasons for action to proper bodies—council
> on ministry. I have an obligation to present national views."

> "Try to look for best alternative—help members find out what is
> possible—then become resource person—help members carry
> out program (want it to be their program rather than mine be-
> cause this increases its chances for success)."

> "Bringing out the Christian perspective in sermons according to
> the Biblical background."

> "The congregation's interest and concern should carry most
> weight in determining social involvement. My role more as pas-
> tor than social activist."

Conflict between clergy and laity is lessened, then, both by
their substantial agreement on the minister's basic role and responsibilities and by the minister's attempts to interpret and
carry out his social action roles in a nonthreatening way. Of
course, some observers would argue that ministers who work
within these bounds are simply yielding to the pressure of their
congregations, that they are nonthreatening because they are
afraid of the personal consequences. Some of the comments of
a sample of California ministers reported by Harold Quinley
(1974b) support this point of view. Although Quinley focused

more on the ministers' personal involvement in political and social action rather than on the local churches' involvement, his
discussion of the social pressures experienced by ministers is
thought provoking in the present context. He describes the process by which career patterns lead those ministers who emerge
from the seminary with idealistic goals into increasingly more
conservative positions on public issues.

> At this point, they experience relatively few cross-pressures over
> their clerical goals and are less settled into their parish positions.
> Like others of the same age, they have smaller families and gen-
> erally have less perceived need to worry about income or job se-
> curity. As they settle into their first jobs, however, they often find
> that their parishioners have very different ideas about the proper
> roles and duties of the cleric. They are "shown the ropes" and
> told that they must conform to certain behavioral norms if they
> hope to succeed in their new position. . . .
>
> The pressures on the young cleric to conform to the wishes of
> his parishioners are great. He has much to gain by playing along;
> much to lose if he does not. His adaptation may be partly con-
> scious—as it was for the California clergymen who told us that
> they avoided certain actions to keep their jobs. Equally often,
> however, it will be an unconscious act, particularly as the new
> minister comes to make friends with the members of his congre-
> gation and to "see" things their way (1974b: 253–254).

Undoubtedly there is truth in Quinley's observation. Yet
there is an alternative explanation of why the strategies of
social-action-oriented ministers changed from the cry of moral
outrage and the confrontation tactics of the 1960s. Quinley
himself detected a growing realization that confrontation tactics
did not necessarily contribute to the long-term solution of public problems. A look back over the 1960s shows that for whatever contribution prophetic preaching made to the national
climate and whatever good it did in bolstering the spirits of civil
rights workers—and these results were considerable and often
of great moment—dramatic actions by individual ministers
often resulted in their being removed from important contexts
where their continued presence was sorely needed.

This point was dramatically illustrated by my study (with Zald, 1966) of a Methodist conference in Alabama. Thirteen of the top 30 churches[5] of the conference were in Birmingham, clearly the center of power of the conference. The bishop resided in Birmingham; principal church-owned institutions were there; the annual meeting of the conference and most of the committee and board meetings were held there. Hence, ministers derived certain advantages from being located in Birmingham, and any appointment took on extra prestige for being in Birmingham. Investigating the hypothesis that there had been an exodus of liberal ministers from the key churches in Birmingham, I asked three conference informants to rate the conservativism or liberalism of a long list of ministers. The list included the pastors over a ten-year period of the 13 churches in Birmingham that were among the top 30 churches of the conference (the most prestigious appointments). The data presented in Table 2.4 indicate that at the beginning of the decade

Table 2.4. Number of Liberal Ministers in the Thirteen Key Birmingham Churches, 1955–1964

| | Minister type | | | |
|---|---|---|---|---|
| | Conservative | Moderate | Liberal | Not able to assign |
| 1955 | 5 | 2 | 5 | 1 |
| 1956 | 5 | 3 | 4 | 1 |
| 1957 | 5 | 3 | 4 | 1 |
| 1958 | 7 | 3 | 3 | 0 |
| 1959 | 8 | 1 | 4 | 0 |
| 1960 | 10 | 1 | 2 | 0 |
| 1961 | 9 | 2 | 1 | 1 |
| 1962 | 9 | 2 | 1 | 1 |
| 1963 | 11 | 1 | 0 | 1 |
| 1964 | 10 | 1 | 0 | 2 |

SOURCE: Adapted from Wood and Zald, 1966.

5. Three criteria were combined in determining the top churches: number of members; amount of minister's salary; and amount contributed to the principal denominational fund (World Service).

the pulpits were held almost evenly by liberals and conservatives but that by the end of the decade the liberals had been forced out.

Such consequences of prophetic preaching did not go unnoticed as ministers faced a changed civil rights context in the 1970s. Once the national witness had been made, ministers might well have decided that it was better to settle in for a long ministry that would attempt to bring the local church along, that is, to involve the local church as a social action agent. This understanding of the church has strong roots in the history of Protestantism. Niebuhr (1956) gave firm intellectual grounding to the role of the "pastoral director," whose primary role is to direct the local church in its ministry to the community. According to Niebuhr, the pastoral director's first function is

> that of building or "edifying" the church; he is concerned in everything that he does to bring into being a people of God who as a Church will serve the purpose of the Church in the local community and the world. Preaching does not become less important for him than it was for the preacher but its aim is somewhat different. It is now pastoral preaching directed toward the instruction, the persuasion, the counseling of persons who are becoming members of the body of Christ and who are carrying on the mission of the Church (1956:82).

Motives for any social action stance are certainly complex, yet my observations support the view that several of the ministers I studied in Indianapolis had consciously adopted the sometimes long-range goal of shaping their churches into social action agents. They seemed genuinely convinced that their liberal causes would be better served by the slow process of leading their churches into social action rather than by more dramatic actions that would represent themselves alone. As we shall see in Chapter 4, many of these ministers led their churches into significant social action that ran counter to the attitudes that members had learned in the community.

## *Summary and Conclusion*

On two issues arising from the core values of the church—racial justice and economic opportunity—members and ministers are sharply divided. Explanations of why there has not been even more conflict on these issues include: members' tendency to shift to churches with ministers whose views are similar to theirs; members' misperception of their ministers' views; members' and ministers' considerable agreement in the areas in which they interact most; members' belief that lay officers have the most influence on social policy; shared norms that give ministers license to disagree with members; ministers' tendency to carry out their social action ministries in a nonthreatening way. My main concern, however, is not with the containment of conflict per se but with the implementation of challenged values. We have seen that the ministers in this study generally shared the values of racial and economic justice that underlie the official policies of the liberal denominations. But the conservative attitudes of members reported in this chapter clearly indicate that local church implementation of the church's values of racial and economic justice is problematic. Some of the factors dampening conflict—specifically, agreement in areas of most interaction, ministers' license to disagree, and nonthreatening strategies—may set the stage for implementation of controversial policies, but, as we shall see, there is much more to the drama. The discussion in Chapter 3 of the sources of attitudes will help us better to understand why some ministers persist in their efforts for these values and why some members oppose those efforts. Chapter 4 will describe and begin the explanation of the extent to which those values were implemented in the sampled local churches.

3
_____

# Sources of Attitudes
# toward Social Issues

Chapter 2 described the range of attitudes toward social issues held by mainline Protestant church members and their ministers and revealed dissension on some issues. The present chapter uses a social interaction perspective to explore the sources of those attitudes and the reasons why ministers and members hold different attitudes. Although these explanations are important in themselves, in this book they serve two further purposes. First, because local churches are voluntary associations, I expect that members' attitudes toward church policies will affect those policies in important ways. Thus, understanding the social network roots of organizational members' attitudes can help us to understand the sources of organizational policy. Similarly, ministers' attitudes also should affect policy, and social networks that influence their views are also sources of church policy. Second, these explanations of attitudes from the perspective of social interaction contribute to our understanding of why members often oppose even those social action policies that derive from the core values of the church.

My argument is that church members who oppose policies based on the core values of the church do so because, in addition to the church's values, they hold contradictory values that are anchored in social interaction outside the church. Ministers, on the other hand, though not immune to outside influences, tend to have both a greater personal investment in the church itself and ideologies that support their loyalty to it. The church's values are more central to their life interests and also are sustained by a social network that helps to keep those values foremost.

## Networks of Social Interaction

Seymour Martin Lipset has written cogently about how networks of social interaction affect the attitudes and behaviors of individuals. His topics have ranged from the authoritarianism of workers to the influence of upper-class status on top-ranking civil servants faced with a newly elected government in Saskatchewan. In *Political Man* he described several elements that contribute to working-class authoritarianism: "low education, low participation in political or voluntary associations of any type, little reading, isolated occupations, economic insecurity, and authoritarian family patterns" (1960: 100). In *Agrarian Socialism* (1950) he illustrated precisely how social interaction can influence the attitudes of individuals:

> The opinion of government officials on the feasibility of any proposal is necessarily colored by their political outlook and by the climate of opinion in their social group. Many top-ranking civil servants in Saskatchewan are members of the upper social class of Regina. Most of their social contacts are with people who believe that they will be adversely affected by many CCF policies. Government officials who belong to professional or economic groups whose position or privileges are threatened by government policies tend to accept the opinion of their own group that reforms which adversely affect the group are wrong and will not work (1950: 321).

Whether individual actions are interpreted in terms of balance theory, reference theory, or some other theory, it makes sense that individuals do not form, develop, and act on attitudes in a vacuum but rather in a network of social interactions.

Without addressing the specific interactions that teach and reinforce values, Dean Hoge's (1976) review of the literature on values suggests that family, career, standard of living, and (where it has been a problem) health are the principal value commitments for Americans generally. The church is seen primarily as a means to these ends. And, as Hoge dramatically illustrates with his analysis of the Angela Davis case, when the church takes actions that threaten these values, commitment to the church is strained.

The task here is to see in the Indianapolis sample of church people the relative impact of church and nonchurch influences on social action attitudes and, more importantly, to compare the relative impact of these influences on members and ministers. The heart of the analysis is based on members' and ministers' own perceptions of the degree of influence exercised on their attitudes by the denomination, by the local church, and by organizations outside the church. First, however, I want to show a wider range of variables affecting attitudes and interpret them in social network terms. These interpretations will help to make us aware of the nature of the argument, which, however, is on firmer empirical ground in the discussion of denominations, local churches, and organizations. Only future research can test the soundness of these interpretations.

VARIABLES RELATED TO BACKGROUND

Church members' attitudes might be rooted in networks of social interaction that could be indexed by such variables as occupation, age, sex, and income. These variables index communalities of values and, by inference, social networks that support these values.

*Age.* To some extent, people born at the same time experience a similar climate of values and type of socialization, leading to what Karl Mannheim (1952) called a collective mentality. In the case of people of different ages, some of their basic values and attitudes were fixed at a different time in the life and history of the social unit to which they belong (Elder, 1975). For example, child-rearing practices have changed from strict to permissive since the Second World War. (Dr. Benjamin Spock's *Baby and Child Care,* with its deliberate attempt to combat rigid child-rearing practices, first appeared in 1946.)

The cohorts of adults who experienced a strict upbringing may differ markedly in their outlook on life from those raised during the permissive period.

Coming of age at a particular point in time also may strongly influence specific attitudes. For example, persons who entered their teens in the early 1960s probably accept church activism more readily than older people because at an impressionable age they were exposed to favorable interpretations by the media, including church publications, of such events as the 1965 march from Selma, Alabama, in which the Reverend Martin Luther King, Jr., and his followers were joined by white church people from across the country.

Finally, the age grouping that is common in American social life means that people of the same age usually reinforce similar attitudes among themselves. Mannheim elaborates the importance of the relation between age and attitudes toward social change:

> That experience goes with age is in many ways an advantage. That, on the other hand, youth lacks experience means a lightening of the ballast for the young; it facilitates their living on in a changing world. One is old primarily in so far as he comes to live within a specific, individually acquired, framework of usable past experience, so that every new experience has its form and its place largely marked out for it in advance. In youth, on the other hand, while life is new, formative forces are just coming into being, and basic attitudes in the process of development can take advantage of the moulding power of new situations (1952:296).

*Education.* Education, here measured by the number of years of school completed, indexes a social network that is important for respondents in this study because of its content and because of the interactions that occur within educational institutions. In both contexts an individual's horizons are broadened beyond the smaller, often closely knit groups of early childhood and family socialization. Furthermore, educated people usually maintain associations with people of like education on a personal basis as well as through literature and other forms of communication. Thus Gabriel Almond and Sidney

Verba (1963) discovered that as the level of educational attainment increases, individuals are more likely to report that they follow politics, pay attention to election campaigns, have more political information, and have opinions on a wider range of political subjects. He or she is more likely to engage in political discussion and with a wider range of people; is more likely to be a member and an active member of some organization; and is more likely to express confidence in his or her social environment and to believe that other people are trustworthy and helpful.

*Income.* Income is an index of a person's stake in society, one's vested interests or lack of them. It also sets or lifts limits on the style of life that one can maintain. For example, income largely determines one's neighborhood—an important center of significant interpersonal relations.

*Occupation.* Occupation also serves as a basis of social interaction in which members are socialized and subject to social control in relation to values that may compete with those of the church. Occupation determines the people with whom an individual associates during most of the day and the nature of that association. Often occupation also affects social interaction off the job.

*Sex.* One's sex indicates the lifelong socialization to which one has been exposed. Sex also restricts one's freedom of association and provides certain vested interests in the rights and privileges of one's sex.

We turn now to those networks of social interaction for which we have members' own judgments about influence on their attitudes toward social action. These variables are the influence of organizations outside the church, the influence of the local church, and the influence of the denomination.

INFLUENCE OF ORGANIZATIONS OUTSIDE THE CHURCH

When we look at organizational memberships as sources of church members' attitudes, the direction of causality is not always certain. Individuals may join organizations because of values they already hold rather than learning the values from these organizations (Bohrnstedt, 1966). Nonetheless, if individuals participate in organizations that support their values, then participation will help to maintain or even intensify those values, because day-to-day application in contemporary situations occurs in a supporting context.

Not satisfied simply to make this inference, I asked church members about the influence of organizations outside the church. Specifically, all members who belonged to organizations outside the church (78 percent of all respondents) were asked, "Of *all* the organizations you belong to (*excluding the church*), which one would you say has the most influence on your attitudes toward social issues?" Thirteen percent responded that none of their organizations influenced their attitudes toward social issues. Surprisingly, 35 percent failed to answer this question (see analyses with this variable below). I was able to classify the organizations reported by the remaining respondents as conservative, liberal, or neutral. Examples of conservative organizations, in order of most mentions, were Masonic lodges, Republican party organizations (including Young Republicans and Republican Women), and the American Legion. Liberal organizations included teachers' unions, Democratic party organizations, and a large variety of social welfare organizations. Parent-teacher organizations, youth-serving organizations (primarily scouting), and civic clubs were the main organizations classified as neutral.

CHURCH INFLUENCES

*Local church influence.* Membership in a particular church whose members have a distinctive mix of attitudes and opinions on social issues may influence a person's views on those issues. As in the case of the other organizations discussed above, a person may join a particular church because of its members' attitudes, that is, may already possess like values before joining. Nevertheless, facing and discussing concrete issues in that context should have some influence.

I constructed two measures based on the members' perceptions of the influence of their local churches, a measure of conservative influence and one of liberal influence. First, I scored local churches as conservative or liberal based on the median social action attitude scale score of its members. (Barton, 1961 : 42, and Tagiuri and Litwin, 1968, discuss variables that measure the climate of values.) Respondents who agreed or strongly agreed with the statement "My local church is an important influence on my attitude toward social issues" were considered to receive conservative influence from their local church if the median scale score of their church was below the median for the sample of churches and liberal influence if their church was above the median.

*Denominational influence.* All the denominations represented in this study had become involved in controversial social action. I had no way to measure directly the influence of these actions and their justifications on the social attitudes of their members. Instead, I measured respondents' perceptions of that influence with the questionnaire item: "My denomination is an important influence on my attitudes toward social issues." Unlike the common denominational affiliation measure, this one meets Norman Blaikie's (1976) standards for the appropriate use of denomination as an explanatory variable.

*Religious beliefs.* The influence of religious beliefs on social attitudes has been a persistent finding in sociological surveys of religious people. Generally, religious beliefs deriving from a literal interpretation of the Bible are associated with conservatism on social issues, while less literal interpretations are associated with social liberalism (Wood, 1967).

It is not easy to describe the social network that is indexed by this variable, because religious beliefs often are learned early in life. These beliefs are more likely related to the larger socioreligious subculture than to the organized church as such (Lenski, 1963 : 332–336).

## Findings on Background Variables

The measure of members' attitudes toward social actions their church might take combines the issues of racial justice, economic opportunity, and the church's involvement in social action. It is a five-item scale based on members' responses to hypothetical actions that might be taken by their local church or its leaders. Cronbach's Alpha for this scale is .74. The five actions are listed below. Possible responses for the first three are listed after the first item; possible responses for the last two items are listed after the fourth item.

> Provided space in the church for meetings of the local chapter of the National Association for the Advancement of Colored People.
>> I would strongly approve.
>> I would approve.
>> I would disapprove.
>> I would strongly disapprove.
>
> Contributed funds to a welfare rights organization.
>
> Publicly *endorsed* busing school children for the purpose of achieving a racial balance in Indianapolis schools.
>
> American churches should provide money for the economic advancement of black Americans.
>> Strongly agree.
>> Agree.
>> Disagree.
>> Strongly disagree.
>
> My local church should concern itself with the problems and needs of its members rather than with social and political problems.

Having specified the variables, I can now state my expectations formally.

*Hypothesis 3.1.*  Church members' attitudes toward social actions their church might take are influenced more by variables outside the church than by church variables.

*Hypothesis 3.2.*  Ministers' attitudes toward social actions their church might take are influenced more by variables inside the church than by outside variables.

Table 3.1 gives the simple correlations of the explanatory variables with the dependent variable, that is, members' attitudes toward social action their churches might take. Only one of the correlations for which I had a specific prediction, that with income, is not statistically significant, and that correlation is in the predicted direction. (Perceived influence by neutral or-

Table 3.1. Correlations between Explanatory Variables and Members' Attitudes toward Social Actions Their Church Might Take

| Explanatory variables | Church members' attitudes toward social action |
|---|---|
| Age | −.18*** |
| Education | .15*** |
| Income | −.03 |
| Occupation | .10*** |
| Sex | .06** |
| Influence of liberal organizations | .17*** |
| Influence of conservative organizations | −.12*** |
| Influence of neutral organizations | −.01 |
| Influence by no organizations | .01 |
| Respondent belongs to no organization | .08*** |
| No answer to the organizational influence question | −.09*** |
| Influence of liberal local church | .11*** |
| Influence of conservative local church | −.08** |
| No influence by a local church | −.05* |
| Influence by the denomination | .09*** |
| Religious beliefs | .17*** |

*p ≤ .05
**p ≤ .01
***p ≤ .001

ganizations and perceived influence by no organizations are dummy variables in the set where my interest is the differential influences of conservative and liberal organizations.)

The first column in Table 3.2 shows that, taken together, the five background variables explain a small, but statistically significant, amount of variation in members' attitudes toward their churches' social action. Age has the strongest effect on these attitudes (net of the other variables), followed by education and income.

Table 3.2. Explaining Church Members' Attitudes toward Social Action (Standardized Coefficients)

| Explanatory variables | Church members' attitudes toward social action | |
|---|---|---|
| Age | $-.16***$ | $-.13***$ |
| Education | $.14***$ | .09 |
| Income | $-.14***$ | $-.12***$ |
| Occupation | $.11***$ | $.09**$ |
| Sex | $.11***$ | $.10***$ |
| Influence of liberal organizations | — | $.19***$ |
| Influence of neutral organizations | — | .06 |
| Influence by no organizations | — | .06 |
| Respondent belongs to no organization | — | $.10**$ |
| No answer to the organizational influence question | — | .02 |
| Influence of liberal local church | — | $.12**$ |
| No influence by a local church | — | .02 |
| Influence by the denomination | — | $.11***$ |
| Religious beliefs | — | $.15***$ |
| R | $.27***$ | $.40***$ |
| $R^2$ | $.07***$ | $.16***$ |

$**p \leqslant .01$
$***p \leqslant .001$

Because I do not have data to establish the specific mechanisms by which these variables affect attitudes, this argument from background variables can only set the stage for a more detailed argument based on organizational memberships. In future research, however, it would be possible to gather detailed data on the social interactions inferred above. For example, the inferences about the influence of age grouping could be checked by asking people detailed questions about the ages and attitudes of the people with whom they interact most.

The 14 explanatory variables, taken together, explain 16 percent of the variation in attitudes (Table 3.2, second column). Only the residual dummy variable categories are not significant. Looking at Table 3.2 from our theoretical perspective, we see that the influence of outside organizations is real. Remembering that the influence of conservative organizations is the reference variable (left out of the regressions) for the set of dummy variables representing organizational influences, we see not only that persons influenced by liberal organizations have significantly more liberal attitudes (in fact, it is the best predictor) but also that persons belonging to no organization at all have significantly more liberal attitudes as well. Hence, our contention that persons opposing church policies derived from church values may do so because of outside influences gains support. (Also note that, although the relationships are not statistically significant, persons who belonged to organizations classified as neutral and those who belonged to organizations but said none influenced their attitudes also had more liberal attitudes than those influenced by conservative organizations.)

The second best predictor of attitudes was religious beliefs, followed by age and income. The next best predictor was influence by a liberal local church, one of the other set of dummy variables. The interpretation is that persons perceiving influence by a local church that is liberal have significantly more liberal attitudes than those who perceive influences by a conservative church. Incidentally, persons who reported that the local church did not influence their attitudes were scarcely more liberal than those influenced by conservative churches.

Of course, the relationships are complex,[1] and much research still needs to be done in order to identify the specific mechanism by which external social networks influence participants in organizations. Nevertheless, the data described thus far generally support the argument that church members' attitudes toward their churches' social policies are rooted at least in part in values learned and supported outside the church. The key question for present purposes is the differential impact on members and ministers of values learned in the church and those learned outside the church.

### Sources of Ministers' and Members' Attitudes Compared

Ministers' attitudes also are influenced by outside socialization and affiliation, but ministers appear to be influenced more than members by values and interactions within the church. For example, 66 percent of the ministers, but only 30 percent of the members, agreed that the denomination had influenced their attitudes toward social issues. Also, 91 percent of the ministers, compared with 62 percent of the members, said that the central interests of their lives were related to the church. Only 4 percent of the ministers, but 20 percent of the members, said that it would not be important at all that their children stay in the same denomination. These findings support Anson Shupe's and my (1973) contention that ministers derive ideologies from their denomination that sustain them when they advocate policies opposed by members.

I have tried in two ways to answer the question: Are ministers and members differentially affected by church influences and outside influences? First, Table 3.3 compares both Bs and Betas for 10 variables. (Of course, ministers in the sample do not vary in occupation; they also do not vary in sex—all are

---

1. Just how complex is clear in Lenski's (1963) contention that religious organizations (he was comparing the major faiths, not churches within Protestantism) become the nucleus for religious subcommunities that may perpetuate values incompatible with the organizations themselves.

males—and they have the same education by my measure. Also, seven of the ministers did not report their income.) The most striking feature of the table is that influence by the denomination is the only significant predictor of ministers' attitudes and that it alone explains more than a fourth of the variation in those attitudes. Moreover, the other three "church" variables also are stronger predictors of ministers' attitudes than they are of members' attitudes. As was true of members, ministers who said they were influenced by their liberal local church had more liberal attitudes than those who said they were influenced by churches that are conservative. That not being influenced by the local church is for ministers a much stronger predictor of liberal attitudes than being influenced by

Table 3.3. Sources of Members' and Ministers' Attitudes toward Church Social Action

| Explanatory variables | Members' attitudes | | Ministers' attitudes | |
|---|---|---|---|---|
| | B | Beta | B | Beta |
| Age | −.32*** | −.15*** | .04 | −.01 |
| Influence of liberal organization | 1.70*** | .20*** | .72 | .11 |
| Influence of neutral organization | .36 | .06 | −.47 | −.07 |
| Influence by no organizations | .62** | .08** | .88 | .11 |
| Respondent belongs to no organizations | .93*** | .15*** | .57 | .08 |
| No answer to the organizational influence question | .33 | .06 | .05 | .01 |
| Influence of liberal local church | .63*** | .11*** | .90 | .15 |
| No influence by a local church | .11 | .02 | 1.86 | .32 |
| Influence by the denomination | .63*** | .11*** | 3.22*** | .52*** |
| Religious beliefs | .09*** | .14*** | .16 | .18 |
| R | | .34*** | | .61** |
| $R^2$ | | .11*** | | .37** |

**p ≤ .01
***p ≤ .001

a liberal church may seem an anomaly, but in fact it makes good sense: even in the liberal churches, the average of members' attitudes is less liberal than the average minister's attitude.

By contrast, outside influences—age and the influence of liberal organizations or belonging to no organizations, as compared with the influence of conservative organizations—are greater for members than for ministers. Both the nonstandardized coefficients (Bs) and the standardized coefficients (Beta weights) suggest the same conclusion: when all the variables are taken into account, the variables that measure the church's influence are markedly more important for ministers than for members. In contrast, the influence of organizations outside the church has more effect on attitudes of members than on those of ministers.

Another way to compare members and ministers is to combine the samples and make ministerial status a variable. Table 3.4 shows that the results of analyses using the combined samples are quite compatible with those reported above. And we see specifically that being a minister is a significant predictor of more liberal attitudes. The table also allows us to look for variables that contribute to ministers' attitudes and for those that mediate the effect of being a minister. It appears that age is a conservative influence on ministers (age is negatively related to liberal attitudes and positively related to ministerial status) but that education is a stronger liberal influence. It also appears that ministers are more susceptible to denominational influence and are more likely to belong to liberal outside organizations— both liberal influences. However, the direct effect of ministerial status on attitudes is stronger than either of these indirect effects.

## Summary and Conclusion

An understanding of members' and ministers' attitudes is important in the organizational analysis of churches because those attitudes help to shape church policies. Generally, the

Table 3.4. Explaining Attitudes toward Social Action (Member and Minister Data Combined)

| Dependent variables | Independent variables[a] | | | | | | | | | |
|---|---|---|---|---|---|---|---|---|---|---|
| | Influence of liberal organizations | Influence by no organizations | Belong to no organizations | Influence of liberal local church | Influence by the denomination | Ministerial status | Age | Education | Beliefs | $R^2$ |
| Influence of liberal organizations | — | — | — | — | — | .07** | .01 | .18*** | .08*** | .05*** |
| Influence by no organizations | — | — | — | — | — | .00 | −.07** | .14*** | −.03 | .02*** |
| Belong to no organizations | — | — | — | — | — | .01 | −.08** | −.19*** | .06* | .03*** |
| Influence of liberal local church | — | — | — | — | — | −.01 | .07** | .03 | −.09*** | .01*** |
| Influence by the denomination | — | — | — | — | — | .10*** | .11*** | −.08*** | −.10*** | .05*** |
| Ministerial status | — | — | — | — | — | — | .05* | .15*** | .02 | .02*** |
| Attitudes toward social action | .19*** | .07* | .16*** | .10** | .12*** | .10*** | −.14*** | .08*** | .13*** | .14*** |

[a]Influence of neutral organizations, no answer, and no influence by a local church are included in the analysis but not shown in order to save space. Their relations to attitudes are not statistically significant.

*p < .05
**p < .01
***p < .001

analyses of this chapter support two basic contentions: attitudes toward the churches' social action are derived from a much larger context than the church, though church influences are important for both members and ministers; and church influences are more important for ministers. These results lend credibility to the argument that members opposing church social action may do so because, in addition to values learned in the church, they, to a larger extent than their ministers, hold contradictory values learned in social interaction outside the church.

# 4

## Churches' Social Action Policies

Both members' and ministers' attitudes toward their churches' social action policies are influenced by social interaction outside the church as well as by interaction within the church. However, one reason that ministers' attitudes are more liberal than members' is that the ministers are more influenced by the church. This chapter shifts the focus from individuals to churches and attempts to discern how local church policies are actually determined. I shall argue that certain social-structural features within the churches affect the ministers' abilities to set policies in accordance with their more liberal attitudes learned and reinforced in the wider church context. The chapter addresses two questions. First, in what ways are the churches involved in social action? Second, what causes this involvement?

Many of the churches' noncontroversial activities are valuable services to segments of the population most affected by social change. For example, consider the actions of the 10 churches that were *least* involved in the controversial issues treated in this study. Five of the churches spent sizable amounts of money on food and clothing for needy families; 3 allowed inner-city 4-H clubs to use church facilities; and 2 were centers for Meals on Wheels, a plan for distributing hot meals to elderly people in the community. In addition, service projects of Sunday school classes and various other groups within the churches involved important one-on-one acts of charity and human kindness.

Yet many church leaders believe that modern society demands something more, specifically, responses that try to change the social milieu that, they believe, is the source of most of the ills of individuals. Indeed, most churches in this study made some such attempt. At least two of them had ministerial staff members assigned primarily to the role of "minister in the community." The following excerpts from the policy statement setting up one of these ministries exemplifies a rationale typical of the most activist churches.

_____ Church has been and is involved in society. Many members are deeply involved through their positions as leaders in business and government. Many more are giving time and talent through the various community agencies and programs. This new ministry is an attempt to build upon these foundations which already exist and to make a more deliberate and concerted effort to mobilize the resources of _____ Church, persons and finances, for ministry in the community. The development of the Ministry of the Church In Community is a means of accepting the challenge and opportunity which we have to be Christ's agent in the world. The primary purpose of this ministry is to involve _____ Church more deliberately and creatively in the community and to help develop a community and world with greater equality and promise for all people. . . .

. . . The fully developed Ministry of the Church In Community will build bridges between the church and the community. The church will be more visible in the community and community needs will be more apparent to the church. It will involve working cooperatively with other churches as well as with public and private agencies. It will necessitate the church's speaking and acting as a corporate entity as it seeks to bring a Christian perspective to other institutions, structures and systems. As the church begins to mobilize and focus its resources in these ways, it becomes more faithful to its mission by "being the good news" as well as by "speaking the good news." In these ways the church accepts the challenge and opportunity to be Christ's agent in the world.

## Forms of Social Action

I measured social action by gathering data on three types of activity: the programs initiated and carried out by a particular church; a church's support of community organizations; and a church's involvement through its denomination's social action program in Indianapolis.

Table 4.1 shows the forms of social action. Local church programs and policies reflect a local church's taking the initiative to aid or champion the cause of some poor or minority group outside the church. Although the actions vary in the degree of controversy they arouse, they express a conviction that individuals are not solely to blame for their misfortunes. This conviction was expressed explicitly in such actions as a church's participation in a demonstration protesting redlining (the refusal of financial institutions to lend money for the purchase of homes in certain neighborhoods). Other actions implied a need to intervene in the social system because it wasn't working properly or justly. For example, inner-city tutoring implied that the inner-city schools were not doing an adequate job.

Direct church support of community organizations that confront controversial issues took such forms as making financial contributions, sending representatives to meetings, recruiting volunteers, and allowing the organizations to use church facilities. One of the active churches kept statistics that suggest the importance of the availability of church facilities for use by outside organizations. During fiscal year 1972–1973 more than 60 community organizations used the church building for a total of 2,990 hours. Even when the largest user, a community preschool, was subtracted, outside organizations used the church's facilities for 1,652 hours—more than three times the number of hours that the building was in use for church activities. As the following statement of policy shows, this church viewed the sharing of its building with community organizations as a major part of its ministry.

> In opening our Church doors and sharing our physical property
> with "non-members" and "non-church organizations" we seek to
> symbolize the opening of our lives as Christians to all men and
> groups regardless of their needs, backgrounds, creedal positions
> or economic status. We offer not our facilities only but our friend
> ship and our corporate resources in the hope of aiding them in

finding meaning and fulfillment in their own relationships and responsibilities as individual citizens, as members of their organizations, and of the larger society of mankind.

A variety of groups, ranging from musical groups to those for transcendental meditation, took advantage of the policy, and a number of them were clearly social action groups, including two racial justice groups, an Appalachian seminar, Hoosiers for Peace, an urban affairs group, and a welfare task force. These groups alone logged 118 hours of building use, about one-fourth the number of hours the building was used for church activities.

The overwhelming support for the Church Federation (see Table 4.1), despite its occasional involvement with issues, reflects its solid acceptance as a multipurpose organization whose goals and activities are for the most part not controversial. (It should be noted, however, that many of the churches belonged to the Church Federation through their denomination.) To some extent, the same is true of social service centers. The members thought of these centers primarily as charitable organizations ministering to individuals in need, even though they also served some advocacy functions.

Denominational officials had argued that some churches would have little direct involvement in social action because they knew that part of the money they gave to the denomination would be used for social action in Indianapolis. For this reason the third measure of participation gave churches credit for supporting activist organizations through their denominations. Much of this support was in the areas of racial justice and welfare rights. One of the major programs drawing denominational support organized sensitivity groups to help whites better understand blacks and thus to prepare whites to accept blacks in their neighborhoods and churches. A center supported by one denomination provided an office for the state welfare rights organization. Although refusal to participate in denominational programs was easier and more frequent in denominations with weak polities, strong-polity churches also sometimes refused to participate.

Table 4.1. Churches' Participation in Social Action

| Form of action | Number of active churches (out of 58) |
|---|---|
| *Local church programs and policies* | |
| Black members (or active recruitment) | 22 |
| Inner-city tutoring (or similar inner-city work) | 16 |
| Liberal stands on such controversial issues as busing, integrated housing, integrated schools, abortion, redlining | 14 |
| Recreation programs for the surrounding neighborhood | 9 |
| Headstart and similar programs | 7 |
| Community forums on controversial issues | 5 |
| "Adoption" of underprivileged children | 5 |
| Thrift shop | 5 |
| Black staff member(s) (other than janitor) | 4 |
| *Direct support of community organizations* | |
| Church Federation | 57 |
| Social service centers | 35 |
| Interracial understanding | 11 |
| Community action programs | 11 |
| Health care centers | 10 |
| Housing opportunity programs | 9 |
| Minority opportunity programs | 7 |
| League of Women Voters | 6 |
| Civil rights organizations | 4 |
| Community improvement associations | 3 |
| *Support for activist organizations through denomination* | |
| Indiana Interreligious Commission on Human Equality (a group sponsoring racial justice programs) | 46 |
| Minority opportunity programs | 9 |
| United Presbyterian Metropolitan Center | 7 |
| Welfare rights organizations | 6 |
| Community action programs | 4 |

In order to have a summary measure of church social action, I added the activities at the three levels, weighting them equally, and assigned a combined social action score to each church. The scores ranged from 1 to 21; the median was 8.88.

## Most Active and Least Active Churches Contrasted

Table 4.1 and the range of summary measures give a good composite picture of the sample churches' social action. That picture will become clearer as the three churches that cluster at the top of the continuum of social action are contrasted with the four churches that cluster at the bottom. The only activities of the four least activist churches that fit my definition of social action were their contributions to the Church Federation. None had programs based on the premise that human misery and need result from anything outside individuals. Although two of the four churches are near heavy concentrations of blacks, none had made an effort to recruit blacks, and no blacks had attended these churches. Apart from the Church Federation, these churches had supported no activist organizations in the community. And, finally, all four of these churches specifically exempted themselves from involvement in their denominations' social action programs.

In contrast, the three most activist churches were highly involved in all three levels of social action. The church with the highest summary social action score decided in 1967 to stay in a racially changing neighborhood and to reach out actively to blacks. Members of the church went door to door inviting blacks to join. After ten years, half of the church's members were black. The church carries on a local program of wide-ranging involvement in health, education, and welfare activities, including employment counseling and community center programs, and the official board has taken liberal public stands, such as endorsement of busing of Indianapolis schoolchildren. Furthermore, the church has given support and cooperation to activist organizations in the community, including the Urban League, the National Association for the Advancement of Colored People, and welfare rights organizations. It has also supported such organizations and activities through its denomination.

The second-ranking church has an open-door policy for blacks, though it had been less active in recruitment. Nonetheless, it had 25 black members, including ushers and choir members, and it had a black professional staff member. Its local program included health and welfare clinics for inner-city residents; for example, the church's classes on cooking and nutrition were attended largely by blacks. This church is actively involved with two other downtown churches in a comprehensive neighborhood development program. It supports a welfare rights organization directly and cooperates in its denomination's support of several activist organizations.

The third church, like the first, lies within a racially changing neighborhood. This church actively recruits blacks but so far has attracted only 20 black members. The leadership of this church was instrumental in founding one of the most activist neighborhood organizations in the city in order to push for open housing and strong, integrated public schools. The church is a member of the association and the site of some of its programs. The official board of the church has strongly advocated integrated housing and schools and it also initiated a campaign against redlining. This church provides the major financial support for its denomination's inner-city community center and also supports the general social action ministry of its denomination.

### Determinants of Local Churches' Social Action

#### MEMBERS' ATTITUDES

What determines the wide variation in social action among the local churches? Despite the literature cited earlier— much of it inspired by Michels—demonstrating that organizations' leaders often are not responsive to members, I expect members' attitudes toward social action to be an important variable in explaining churches' social action. One important reason for this hypothesis is that the issues studied here are controversial and therefore likely to stir members from their apathy (Wood, 1970). If members of any voluntary association are genuinely interested in influencing policy, they probably can do so—especially if they have time or other resources to spend for that influence.

The averages for each church that were derived from the scales of members' attitudes toward social action that their church could take (described in Chapter 3) permit a test of this hypothesis. A continuation of our contrast between the most and least activist churches gives a hint to what we shall find. On social action with regard to racial issues, there is a clear contrast between members of the most activist churches (where the mean of members' attitudes in each of the three churches was above the mean for the whole sample of churches) and members of the least activist churches (where the mean for members in three of the four churches was below the grand mean). When the issue is economic opportunity, the picture is not so clear. In the top three churches, members are above the mean in one, at the mean in another, and slightly below the mean in a third. In the bottom churches, members are below the mean in two churches and above the mean in two.

### FORMAL LEGITIMACY

I also hypothesize that leaders' formal legitimacy and members' belief in legitimacy (see the discussion of these concepts in Chapter 1) will restrict, or at least filter and shape, the influence of members' attitudes on policy. Formal legitimacy may insulate leaders to some extent from pressure by members, depending on the roles and rights of leaders that are built into the organization's formal structure (for example, the constitution and bylaws). According to Stinchcombe (1968), leaders with formal legitimacy can carry out those actions allowed to them by the law of the organization and often backed up by the law of the state. There are often specified limits on leaders, providing, if not a guide, at least a boundary to their actions. On the other hand, as long as leaders stay within those boundaries, there are nests of power, whether organizational or extra-organizational, that can be called on to put down their challengers. Indeed, as long as the legal structure remains intact, it is not necessary for those affected by the actions to assent to them, even though they may do so for a variety of reasons, not the least of which might be their knowledge that leaders have more power to back up their actions than the members could muster to counter them.

For example, consider whether local churches would accept blacks as members. I expect that local churches' efforts to integrate their membership will transcend their members' attitudes toward integration more often in denominations that give leaders formal legitimacy than in denominations that do not. Denominations with formal legitimacy can enact binding canons or issue authoritative directives. They may also subject non-complying churches to denominational sanctions, for example, official censure or refusal to loan money for buildings, and in some cases noncomplying members can be excommunicated. In denominations without formal legitimacy, leaders can only use moral suasion.

In the present study formal legitimacy is measured as a dichotomy between denominations in which the local church owns its own property and can hire and fire its own minister and denominations in which one or both of these rights is formally located at a point in the denominational structure above the local church (Wood, 1970). All three of the most activist churches are in denominations where formal legitimacy is strong; three of the four least activist churches are in denominations with weak formal legitimacy.

BELIEF IN LEGITIMACY

Belief in legitimacy refers to members' belief that leaders' decisions should be accepted despite personal disagreement. This concept is extracted from Weber's (1968) classic analysis. Weber understood legitimacy as a means of securing voluntary cooperation of the persons actually affected by the actions. Leaders believe in their legitimacy on some basis and use it as their basis for claiming members' support. Members who believe that leaders are legitimate are less likely to challenge their decisions seriously. Two items from the belief in legitimacy scale will show the concept's essential meaning (see Appendix A for the entire scale): "Even when I disagree, I feel a moral obligation to support the social policies of my denomination"; "If policies of my local church and denomination were in conflict on some issue, I would feel obligated to follow the denomination's policies." Looking at mean scores for members' belief in legitimacy, we find that two of the three top churches have members above the grand mean, and all four of the bottom churches have members below the grand mean.

### LOCAL CHURCH BUDGET

I expected size of the budget to predict local church social action not only because such action often costs money but also because small budgets are less likely to have discretionary items. (Campbell and Pettigrew, 1959, found that financial campaigns for large amounts could also have a conservative effect, however.) The rationale for expecting financially secure churches to engage in more social action is more fully discussed in Chapter 5. The most and least activist churches can be contrasted on the size of their budgets and thus on the economic resources potentially available for social action and on their security when facing controversy. The contrast is striking: the average budget for the three most activist churches was $162,624, contrasted with an average budget of $53,754 for the least activist churches. But the correlation between size of budget and involvement in social action is not perfect: the most activist church had a budget smaller than those of three of the least activist churches.

### ATTITUDES OF MINISTERS AND LAY LEADERS

From Michels's perspective that leaders have illicit control and from the perspective of legitimate control, the attitudes of the minister and, to a lesser extent, those of lay officers should affect a church's involvement in social action. To evaluate this expectation, I used scales for ministers and lay officers that are comparable to the attitude scale for members (see Appendix A). A comparison of the sets of churches with regard to their officers' attitudes toward social action for racial justice offers exactly the same result as the comparison of their members' attitudes: officers' attitudes in the three top churches were above the grand mean; officers' attitudes in three of the bottom four churches were below the grand mean. On economic opportunity issues, the contrast is slightly sharper. In three of the four bottom churches (compared with two of the four for members) the mean of officers' attitudes is below the mean of all the officers in the sample. The sharpest contrast between these sets of churches is on their ministers' attitudes toward social action. On issues of both racial justice and economic opportunity, the ministers of the three top churches are all above the mean for the ministers in the sample. In the bottom churches, three of the four ministers are below the mean on racial attitudes, and two of them are below the mean on economic attitudes as well.

The contrast on officers' belief in legitimacy is exactly the same as that for members: in two of the three top churches officers' attitudes are above the grand mean, and in all four of the bottom churches officers' attitudes are below the grand mean. All three of the ministers in the most activist churches rate above the mean for ministers' belief in legitimacy. Only one of the four ministers in the least activist churches rated above the mean.

FINDINGS

All six of the variables discussed here and listed in Table 4.2 affect the social action of local churches, but formal legitimacy, members' attitudes, and ministers' attitudes have much stronger correlations (see Table 4.2, column 1). Both belief in legitimacy and lay officers' attitudes correlate relatively weakly. Regression analysis using all these variables shows that formal legitimacy, members' attitudes, and size of the budget are the most power-

Table 4.2. Major Variables Explaining Variation in Churches' Social Action

| Variable | Combined social action score | |
| --- | --- | --- |
| | $r$ | Beta |
| Formal legitimacy | .52** | .33** |
| Members' attitudes | .47** | .30* |
| Size of budget | .28* | .28* |
| Belief in legitimacy | .17 | .09 |
| Ministers' attitudes | .45** | .16 |
| Lay officers' attitudes | .19 | .02 |
| R | | .70** |
| $R^2$ | | .48** |

*$p < .05$
**$p < .01$

ful predictors (see column 2). The other variables do not have an independent, statistically significant effect on the social action of local churches. Together, these variables explain 48 percent of the variation in social action.

## Summary and Conclusion

In this chapter I have illustrated how Indianapolis churches attempted to change their social milieu. Several churches initiated programs designed to change Indianapolis by increasing racial integration, creating new opportunities for the poor, and ensuring the civil rights of all citizens. A few churches may even themselves be characterized as social action organizations, or, at least, they have built social action units prominently into their internal structure. All but one of the churches gave some direct support to at least one community organization outside the church. And most of the churches also supported one or more such organizations through their denominations. I described a summary measure of church social action and compared in detail the churches that scored highest on that measure with those that scored lowest.

Finally, I discussed six possible determinants of differences in churches' social action: members' attitudes; formal legitimacy; belief in legitimacy; size of budget; ministers' attitudes; and lay leaders' attitudes. Statistical analyses showed that all six variables affected the social action of churches but that three of them—formal legitimacy, members' attitudes, and budget—were most useful in explaining churches' social action.

Michels's analysis nothwithstanding, the great influence that members exercise on local churches' social action policies is not surprising. These policies are visible and often affect members directly; moreover members hold the purse strings. What remains problematic is leaders' ability to implement policies that transcend members' preferences. Organizational transcendence and the legitimate means of achieving it are the subjects of Chapter 5.

# 5

## Legitimate Leadership and Controversial Policies

Organizational transcendence occurs when an organization uses its name and other resources in actions not predictable from its members' attitudes toward those actions. Transcendence results from the exercise of social control and can exist even when the opposed members are fully aware of the policies. Michels believed that oligarchy—an illegitimate form of transcendence—would inevitably develop in every organization, but I have argued that transcendence can be legitimate under certain conditions (see Chapter 1). This chapter first identifies transcendence among the sampled churches, then explores the conditions that allow leaders to implement policies transcending members' preferences.

### Measuring Transcendence

Were any of the sampled churches more active than would have been predicted on the basis of their members' attitudes? More specifically, had they become involved despite potentially strong opposition from members? When mechanisms of social control are effective, local churches' policies and actions may go counter to the average of their members' personal views, even with the members' full knowledge of what is happening.

To assess the degree of transcendence on social action issues, I devised scores that compared the actual social actions of each church with members' approval or disapproval of possible actions by their local church, such as contributing funds to a welfare rights organization. The scores were determined by a comparison for each church of the members' attitudes and the church's action on five issues that had in fact resulted in actions by some of the churches or by organizations they supported. For the five questionnaire items and the possible responses, see p. 50. It seems plausible to assume that members who agree with the statement "My local church should concern itself with the problems and needs of its members rather than with social and political problems" do not want their churches either to engage in or to support activist organizations.

The transcendence score for each church was determined by: finding what actions, if any, a church had taken despite opposition (inferred from attitudes)[1] from at least 50 percent of its members (if a church had taken no such actions, its score was zero); subtracting 50 from the percentage opposed to each action; and adding up the remainders across issues. The transcendence scores ranged from 0 to 142; the median was 16. Twenty-two churches—40 percent of the sample—did not transcend their members, but 60 percent did. Table 5.1 uses data on the most and least involved churches to illustrate measurement of transcendence on the issue of welfare rights. The transcendence scores used in the following analyses result from adding up the transcendence scores on several issues related to equality of economic opportunity and racial justice.

## *The Importance of Transcendence*

The importance of church leaders' ability to commit resources for the advancement of other groups can be dramatically illustrated on the national level. Both Senator Hubert Humphrey, who was for it, and Senator Richard Russell, who was against it, credited the passage of the 1964 civil rights bill to the persistence of church pressure (Spike, 1965). More re-

1. It would have been better to have a stronger measure, such as members' votes on issues, but these were not available. In many cases issues were not voted on.

Table 5.1.  Measuring Transcendence on Welfare Rights Issues

| Local church | Percentage of members disapproving support of welfare rights | Church position | Degree of transcendence on welfare rights |
|---|---|---|---|
| Most Active | | | |
| A | 49 | Support | 0 |
| B | 57 | Support | 7 |
| C | 65 | Support | 15 |
| Least Active | | | |
| D | 59 | No Support | 0 |
| E | 68 | No Support | 0 |
| F | 70 | No Support | 0 |
| G | 83 | No Support | 0 |

cently, the liberal churches were part of a coalition of established organizations sponsoring the activities of the United Farm Workers (UFW). The importance of support from established organizations is seen not only in the success of the UFW but also in the dismal future of insurgent efforts without such support. J. Craig Jenkins and Charles Perrow (1977) conclude their description of the contributions of the sponsoring organizations to the success of UFW with the observation that "there is the possibility of abandonment. Since liberal support can fade and political elites shift their stance, as has happened to the UFW since 1972, even the gains of the past may be endangered" (1977:267–268). They suggest that groups excluded from American politics are in a precarious position.

A look back at Table 4.1 gives an idea of the difference it would make at the local level if leaders were unable to overcome resistance of members to the championing of underprivileged groups in our society. Support for groups represented by minority opportunity programs, civil rights organizations, inner-city improvement associations, and welfare rights organizations appears particularly precarious.

## *Legitimate Control and Transcendence*

Church members' attitudes toward social issues and toward their local churches' response to those issues are important determinants of churches' social action. But a church's behavior is not totally explainable in terms of its members' attitudes and the external social forces that have shaped those attitudes. Most of the churches studied have become involved in social action to an extent that could not have been predicted from knowledge of their members' attitudes toward social action. The remainder of this chapter explores possible explanations for this transcendence. I argue that a church's transcendence of attitudes that members derive from outside the church is often a legitimate consequence of agreed-upon social structures and social values. My concern with legitimate transcendence leads to hypotheses that use formal legitimacy and belief in legitimacy to explain transcendence and that allow the assessment of both alternative and supplementary explanations.

FORMAL LEGITIMACY

As noted in Chapters 1 and 4, legitimacy can be objective, that is, embodied in previously agreed-upon understandings, or it can be subjective, that is, based on a feeling of obligation. The former type is usually reflected in formal documents, such as a constitution or bylaws. Where such documents give leaders powers to act independently of the membership, they are an important resource for transcendence.

*Hypothesis 5.1.* A local church's transcendence of its members' attitudes toward social issues varies directly with the degree of formal legitimacy in its denomination.

BELIEF IN LEGITIMACY

Because churches are voluntary organizations, the extent of their formal control over members is severely limited. Belief in legitimacy (Weber, 1968) refers to members' sense of a deep-seated moral obligation to support policies that derive from a particular source, regardless of the organization's formal legitimacy. Members who believe in the legitimacy of leaders' actions probably will support them voluntarily.

*Hypothesis 5.2.* Local churches' transcendence of members' attitudes toward social issues varies directly with members' belief in the legitimacy of denominational control.

Theoretically, strong belief in legitimacy could exist independent of formal legitimacy. However, data from the pilot project (Wood, 1975) for this study indicated that for mainline Protestant churches belief in legitimacy is associated with formal legitimacy and that belief mediates formal legitimacy's effect on transcendence.

TOLERANCE OF DISSONANT POLICY

An additional concept that might mediate the effect of belief in legitimacy is tolerance of dissonant policy. When most members feel a moral obligation to support their leaders, then not only they but also those members who do not believe in the legitimacy of leaders' actions are subject to social pressures that make defiance difficult (Bierstedt, 1954:81; Nisbet, 1970:113–118; Blau, 1964:chap. 8). Of all the conditions that permit transcendence, members' tolerance of dissonant policy may be the most critical. I use the concept as an extension of the concept of compliance. If compliance is defined as behaving in accordance with a directive from the leader of one's organization (compare Etzioni, 1961:3), then tolerance can be defined as failing to protest strenuously despite awareness that the name and resources of one's organization are being used in ways that one does not approve.[2] The relationship between control struc-

---

2. In its function, tolerance is akin to trust (Gamson, 1968). However, trust implies a belief that leaders will not use resources in ways the member does not approve, whereas tolerance implies that the member accepts the fact that leaders sometimes must use resources in ways the member disapproves.

ture and tolerance is indicated by substituting the concept of
tolerance for that of compliance in a paraphrase of Peter Blau:
"The institutionalization of authority requires that the social
norms that demand [tolerance of organizations'] policies and
the surrounding values that justify and reinforce this [toler-
ance] become part of the common culture and be transmitted
from generation to generation" (1964 : 211).

I have measured tolerance of dissonant policy as follows. Ev-
eryone who disapproved or strongly disapproved of any of 17
possible local church policies (for example, "Publicly *endorsed*
busing of school children for the purpose of achieving a racial
balance in Indianapolis schools"; "Publicly *opposed* busing of
school children for the purpose of achieving a racial balance in
Indianapolis schools") was asked, "Which *one* of the following
is the *strongest* expression of disapproval you would be willing
to make (if necessary) in this instance?" Tolerance ranged from
"I would *not* openly express my disapproval in this instance"
(most tolerant) to "withhold donations and pledges" or "join another local church" (least tolerant). Details about the scale are
included in Appendix A.

Tolerance of dissonant policy may intervene between legitimacy and transcendence; that is, where leadership is bolstered
by belief in its legitimacy, members are more likely to tolerate
dissonant policies.

*Hypothesis 5.3.* Members' tolerance of dissonant policy varies
directly with belief in legitimacy, *and*

*Hypothesis 5.4.* Members' tolerance of dissonant policy varies
directly with transcendence.

MINISTERS' BELIEF IN LEGITIMACY

A denomination's control structure affects the local church
by defining the role and powers of the minister. Thus the institutionalized power structure may affect transcendence by influencing a minister's concept of his role. Following Weber
(1968), I expected that the control system would not rely solely

on material advantage (for example, a secure career) to obtain the loyalty of ministers but would also attempt to cultivate in them a belief in the system's legitimacy and thus belief in their legitimacy as an administrative staff. Leaders generally are more liberal than their followers (Stouffer, 1963), and my data (see Chapter 2) corroborate Jeffrey Hadden's (1969) demonstration that ministers are more liberal than church members. Here, however, we are concerned with the inclination of ministers to translate their desires into local church policy.

Mayer Zald and Patricia Denton (1963) found that YMCA secretaries had developed an "ideology of lay control" that caused them not to initiate policies that were out of line with lay wishes. Ministers in denominations with weak polities have probably developed similar ideologies; conversely, ministers in strong polities have probably developed an ideology of clerical control. It can be expected, then, that the tendency to initiate policy not desired by a substantial proportion of the membership will vary with the formal legitimacy of the denomination. Thus, a minister's belief in the legitimacy of denominational control, including the legitimacy of his own role as administrator of that control, may be an intervening variable that mediates the effect of formal legitimacy on a local church's transcendence of its members' attitudes.

*Hypothesis 5.5.* Formal legitimacy is positively related to ministers' belief in legitimacy, *and*

*Hypothesis 5.6.* Ministers' belief in legitimacy is positively related to transcendence.

The scale for ministers' belief in legitimacy contained twelve items, including "It is not right for a local church to disregard the counsel of denominational leaders" and "My first loyalty is to my local church, not to the denomination." See Appendix A for the complete scale.

In summary, formal legitimacy is a source of transcendence because it entails strong sanctions and the threat of their use. It is indirectly related to transcendence because organizations in which leaders have formal legitimacy tend to instill supporting ideologies (belief in legitimacy) in both members and leaders.

## Other Interpretations of Transcendence

An alternative explanation of transcendence derives from Michels's discussion of his iron law of oligarchy. According to this explanation, transcendence is not legitimate but exists primarily because leaders take advantage of members' apathy.[3]

I used two techniques to ensure that apathy would not distort my findings on the legitimacy of transcendence. First, I chose issues that had high salience in our society. Indeed, the majority of members in each of the sampled churches disapproved of church involvement of the kind and extent discussed in this chapter. Second, I devised a scale to measure members' apathy and employed this measure as a control variable in the statistical analysis. Two items from the questionnaire indicate the type of attitude I was trying to isolate (Appendix A shows the entire eight-item scale): "The central interests of my life are not closely related to the church"; "To be perfectly honest, I don't care what my local church says or does about social issues."

Another explanation of transcendence contends that secure organizations are in a better position to take risks. Betty Boyd Roe and I (1975) demonstrated that college sororities could use appropriate innovations to meet crises created by a changing environment if they had the security derived from prestige, success at recruitment, or financial solvency. In the sorority study solvency was measured by subtracting the estimated annual operating expenses from the estimated annual operating income and then subtracting the annual mortgage payment. Those sororities with a financial surplus were more likely to adopt housing policies that ran some risk of decreasing income

3. See Chapter 1 for my argument that Michels's other explanations of oligarchy (for example, the incompetence of the masses) are less applicable to contemporary society.

(for example, allowing members some freedom to live outside the sorority house) but that would facilitate recruitment of desired prospects who are esteemed in the larger university community. Sororities without a financial surplus were more likely to require all members to live in the house, even though this requirement hindered recruitment of some of the women they most wanted.

Financially insecure churches also experience policy constraints. In their study of ministers' responses to the racial crises in Little Rock, Arkansas, Ernest Campbell and Thomas Pettigrew (1959) found that financial considerations influenced social action policy. The ministers whose churches were engaged in building or financial campaigns were less likely to speak out for integration. Campbell and Pettigrew reasoned that size of budget and number of members symbolized many of the criteria by which ministers are judged. Ministers believed that prophetic preaching was important, but not of such overriding importance that they could risk failure in these two important areas.

Applying this reasoning to the present study, I would add that many of the kinds of social action studied here cost money. Thus, a church that had most of its resources committed to salaries and building maintenance would have little left to spend on social action even if its members desired such action. It should also be noted that a minister who is clearly successful in recruiting members and raising funds is likely to have considerable good will and respect to fall back on when he involves the church in controversial activities.

In this study both the size of the annual budget and the number of members are indicators of organizational security. An explanation based on organizational security could supplement either of the two explanations proposed above. That is, Michels argued that control of organizational resources is a principal means by which leaders acquire and maintain illegitimate control; however, organizational resources could also be used for legitimate control.

### Testing a Model of Organizational Transcendence

Chapter 4 showed that 38 of the 58 sampled churches (66 percent) had transcended their members' attitudes toward church involvement in controversial social issues. In a formal theoretical model (Figure 5.1) three variables mediate the effect of formal legitimacy on transcendence: minister's belief in legitimacy; members' belief in legitimacy; and members' tolerance of policies with which they do not agree. The church's budget also is an important independent variable. Apathy is significantly related to transcendence only through a negative relation with tolerance of dissonant policies. Hence, contrary to the implications of Michels's work, those for whom the organiza-

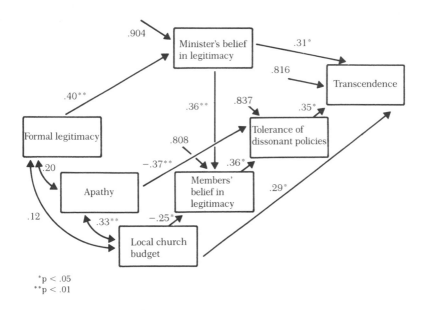

*p < .05
**p < .01

Figure 5.1.
Legitimacy as a Source of Transcendence

tion was least salient were least likely to tolerate social policies with which they disagreed. For them, presumably, the costs of changing organizations are not great or the feeling of obligation to continue monetary support is not strong.

Because both kinds of legitimacy are related to transcendence as predicted by the model, and because apathy is not related in the way Michels implied, the argument made at the beginning of this chapter is supported: a church's transcendence of attitudes that members derive from outside the church is often a legitimate consequence of agreed-upon social structures and social values. (It should be noted that structural security also directly affects transcendence.) Weber's work is more helpful than Michels's in explaining transcendence in these organizations. The mediating effects of ministers' and members' belief in the legitimacy of the national organization support Weber's (1968) contention that leaders would not rely on formal sanctions alone but would attempt to instill in their followers a belief in the legitimacy of the administrative structure. The link between tolerance and belief in legitimacy supports Weber's expectation that belief in legitimacy would assure voluntary compliance with administrative direction. Belief in legitimacy is important not only because coercive incentives are costly (for example, the necessary supervision of participants) but also because they tend to alienate members (Etzioni, 1961; Simon, 1965). Voluntary organizations, moreover, cannot coerce even minimum behavior if the participant is willing to accept expulsion from the organization. Even organizations with substantial formal legitimacy need to cultivate or maintain belief in legitimacy in order to assure voluntary support.

Once established, formal legitimacy provides resources and mechanisms that tend to maintain the belief in legitimacy. Such a mechanism is the hierarchical control of church school teaching materials. In strong formal polities the national leadership has more formal authority both to develop such materials and to ensure that they are used. Consider also how formal legitimacy helps to preserve traditional belief by controlling schisms. When controversy occurs, resistance is mobilized rapidly until it reaches an apex, then it begins to decay. In churches with weak polities, decisions can be made while resistance is at its peak; for example, a Baptist church can dismiss its minister or disaffiliate from the national body in two weeks or less. Those churches with stronger polities must follow relatively long, drawn-out procedures that give time for heads to cool and sober second thoughts to develop (Stouffer, 1963). Thus, churches with stronger polities can better withstand the threat of widespread erosion of belief in legitimacy (Wood, 1975).

## Summary and Conclusion

Michels's iron law of oligarchy implies that organizational policies out of line with members' attitudes necessarily constitute displacement of organizational goals by leaders pursuing their vested interests; hence, such policies and such leadership are not legitimate. On the contrary, I have suggested that such policies may be legitimate when members voluntarily subject themselves to a formal system of control that they believe has the right to coerce the surrender of their wishes to established goals of the organization (formal legitimacy) or where members voluntarily support dissonant policies because they believe that they should do so (belief in legitimacy).

In the analysis thus far, I have assumed that the claim to legitimacy is based on legality or rationality or both, and this assumption has received support. However, as I read church materials and talked with leaders, I became convinced that another basis for the claim was also important: leaders seemed to claim legitimacy for their policies on the grounds that these actions were derived from the core values of the church. A value-based claim to legitimacy is consistent both with nonthreatening leadership strategies and with the need for voluntary compliance. Chapter 6 lays the groundwork for a theory of legitimate leadership based on organizational values.

*6*

---

# A Theory of Legitimate Leadership in Voluntary Organizations

There is no simple reason why churches continue to participate in social action despite members' opposition. Many social forces combined to commit most large national church bodies to liberal positions on social issues (Hadden, 1969; Quinley, 1974a; Wood, 1967, 1972b), and interaction with national leaders influenced many ministers and lay leaders to share that commitment. Certain structural arrangements allowed leaders to determine policy (Wood, 1970, 1972a), and ideological factors allowed the leaders to persist despite resistance (Shupe and Wood, 1973). Eventually, the value climate in the church allowed leaders to persuade many lay people to support controversial social policies and many more to tolerate them. The role of values was crucial: leaders interpreted social change against the stable values of the church—values already in the value repertoire of members—and were able to heighten members' awareness of those values as they assessed church policies. This interpretation will be elaborated here as a rudimentary theory of legitimate leadership in voluntary organizations.

## Values as a Source of Belief in Legitimacy

This study shows that formal legitimacy is an important factor in members' acceptance of disliked policies but that it does not stand alone. When members disapprove of a particular policy, they need more than to know that leaders have the

84

power to enforce it anyway (unless members mobilize extraordinary resources); they also need to believe that somehow *the action* is right. The study suggests that a belief in legitimacy helps members to tolerate new policies that are inconsistent with attitudes they have learned from networks of social interaction outside the church and that this tolerance allows transcendence. But precisely what mechanisms allow belief in legitimacy to have this effect?

The measure of belief in legitimacy employed here tapped a deep-seated obligation to accept policies set by the denomination. Undoubtedly, members feel this obligation in part because of their belief in the right of duly elected leaders to set policy (Gamson, 1968). Certainly in the 1960s the Southern Presbyterian Church based one of its claims to legitimacy on this point with some success (Wood, 1975). However, another basis of legitimacy is becoming increasingly important. When issues are given wide publicity in the media, members are more likely to pay attention to the actual content of policy. Thus, an effective claim to legitimacy must tie the content of policy to the major goals and values of the organization.

My view is that organizations, or at least the type that I have called value-fostering organizations, are based on fundamental values that can provide the legitimacy for organizational actions. (In addition to religious groups, value-fostering organizations include patriotic societies, civil rights organizations, political parties, and labor unions.) In the case of religious organizations, leaders frame policies on social action to reflect the fundamental values of the church, such as Biblically based concepts depicting the church as the servant of a just and compassionate God. They then use those values as a basis for claiming legitimacy for controversial policies by bringing to consciousness the members' belief in those general values—thus raising the rank of those values within members' value hierarchies (Rokeach, 1973)—and by encouraging members to apply the general values to the specific policies.

In deriving specific policies from general values, leaders are engaging in a process that anthropologists call sanctification (see the discussion of Rappaport, 1971, below) and that sociologists call the social construction of reality. As Peter Berger and Thomas Luckmann have suggested (1966:94), the fundamental legitimating explanations are built into the vocabulary of faith (for example, the fatherhood of God and the brotherhood of man). But to establish a link between general values and a specific policy, such as busing or contributing to a welfare rights organization, involves a new construction of reality. Murray Edelman saw this clearly: "If legislative, administrative, and judicial procedures significantly influence how people see leaders, issues, and themselves, then those procedures are less likely to reflect the people's will than to shape it. More precisely, they reflect it only after they shape it" (1971:175).[1] In contrast to broader political processes, however, value-fostering organizations such as the church have a more central set of values to which members have been socialized and of which they are continually reminded, for example, through the use of the Bible and of Biblically based rituals in weekly services. Thus, at least in a general sense (often embedded in Jesus' parables or in descriptions of events in his life), these values are well known among church members. Hence leaders have these Biblical values as reasonably clear guides to the way in which they shape the will of the people and as a basis for shaping that will.

This process of building legitimacy on the basis of shared values is reflected in the report of the 1971 convention of the Christian Church (Disciples of Christ):

> Whereas the Christian Faith calls persons to develop and use those talents with which they have been endowed, so long as those talents are consistent with Christian values and tradition; and
> Whereas our system of mass public education seems at times to contradict this principle by regimenting children and youth into patterns of mass behavior that may be inconsistent both with the

---

1. Apparently Edelman and I view this fact differently. He stresses the possibility that people are being duped; I stress the possibility that they are being led.

principles of individual development and the principles of the
Christian faith; and
Whereas the Christian faith affirms that all persons are entitled
to equal opportunity for self-development regardless of their race,
economic status or home situation; and
Whereas it has been shown that most public schools located in
low-income and minority neighborhoods do not provide such
equal opportunity to their pupils (Owen, 1972).

The report goes on to call for concern for the equality of public
school education and support of programs designed to overcome racial imbalance, such as "busing of students, redistrict-
ing of schools, transfer of teachers, etc."

One of the churches sampled in the present study provided
an information leaflet for visitors to the church. The following
is one of twelve paragraphs that describe what it means to be a
member of the church:

A willingness to strive to see the problems and needs of the
world, the nation, and the community—problems of economics,
politics, culture, and morals—through the eyes of Christ, in
other words, to try to look at our problems not just as an American, or as a [member of this denomination], or as a man or
woman, or as a member of a certain neighborhood, or a certain
economic or professional group, but as a *Christian.* This may
involve asking oneself the simple question: "How can I best
serve Jesus Christ in this particular situation?" A Christian,
therefore, needs to study all sides of a debatable issue. A Christian needs to be *informed.* Above all, the Christian should be
Biblically informed.

A final illustration of this process of raising members' consciousness of the church's values as they consider controversial
issues paraphrases a statement by a minister in a racially
changing neighborhood who was dealing with his board's reluc-
tance to face the issue of racial integration.

The question has arisen whether we foresee the time we will
welcome people of other racial groups. This question cannot be
answered today, but I do want to indicate additional questions

raised by this one: 1) What does the New Testament say about
Christian faith expressed in race relationships? 2) How would
Jesus answer the matter of racial attitudes and race relationships? 3) Is the church in the first place "Christ's church," or,
do we consider it as "our church primarily"? What are some of
the conclusions to be drawn in each answer? As your pastor, I
present these questions to which I hope you will give serious
thought, study, and prayer.

These illustrations are only a sample of the materials that
revealed the value-based claim for the legitimacy of social action. This evidence suggested the need for a variable that would
reflect whether ministers were linking social action to the core
values of the church. The first question in the ministers' interview had been: "What image do you most want your church to
have in the minds of (1) your members? (2) people in the community?" I measured the claim to legitimacy of social action by
whether a minister included social action in the image he most
wanted his church to have. I reasoned that making social action a part of the church's primary image would necessarily require relating it to the fundamental values of the church. (For a
discussion of image projection as a social control device, see
Gamson, 1968: 118–119.) In fact, in answering this question
or later questions (such as: "How do you perceive *your* role
in formulating social policy?"), each of the 21 ministers who
had linked social action to his church's image also used some
phrase that indicated a conscious relating of core values to social action. The phrases they used included: "the application of
scripture to life"; "loyalty to Christ"; "an expression of faith";
"in the name of Christ"; and "living Christian lives."

## Discussion of Findings

I expected that ministers' attempts to create an image
of social action for the church would increase transcendence,
partly because such attempts would force members to judge
the church's social action by the church's values as well as
by those of their other social networks. Therefore, I expected

to find more belief in the legitimacy of social action among members of churches whose ministers tied such action to the church's core values.[2]

Figure 6.1 shows that the expected result appeared. In churches where the minister expressed a desire that the church project a social action image, I observed a higher level of members' belief in legitimacy. The increased belief in legitimacy, in turn, increased transcendence indirectly through tolerance of dissonant policy. (Of course, the relatively strong direct relation between minister's desire and transcendence evidences the need for continued study of the wider sources of ministers' influence.)[3]

This argument needs rigorous testing. Future research should pay special attention to whether other forms of legitimacy free the minister to strengthen his position with legitimacy derived from core values or whether core-value legitimacy may be effectively used to shore up eroding legitimacy of other types.

2. Of course, with this measure I cannot rule out the possibility that ministers see a social action image as possible because of their members' belief in legitimacy. In future research, content analysis of a minister's sermons, reports to the congregation, and membership recruitment materials might provide better measures of a claim to legitimacy based on core values. Even such measures could not rule out entirely the possibility that the minister would link social action to core values partly because he or she knew in advance that such a claim would be credited.

3. Figure 6.1 shows a negative, though not statistically significant, relation between minister's desire for a social action image and tolerance for dissonant policy. A plausible interpretation for such a finding is that a vigorous claim that social action springs from the core values of the church can cause backlash among members who reject the claim. Thus, ministers who were trying to create an image of social action were waving a red flag at members, causing them to worry about the imagined consequences of potential policies. But where the claim to legitimacy is accepted, there should be less alarm. To check this interpretation, I divided the sample into churches that were above the median on belief in legitimacy and those that were below the median. I expected that in the churches with a high level of belief in legitimacy the negative relation between image and tolerance would be greatly reduced or disappear. And in fact, the relationship was greatly reduced. There were too few cases to allow me to settle the matter with this sample, but the hypothesis is a fruitful one for future research.

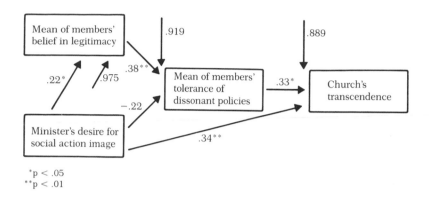

*p < .05
**p < .01

Figure 6.1.
Minister's Desire for Social Action Image
Increases Members' Belief in Legitimacy


Nevertheless, the data support the hypothesis that once policies are disputed, leaders can increase belief in legitimacy by linking challenged policies to core values. As the minister raises members' consciousness of the church's values in relation to community issues, members can more easily believe in the legitimacy of both local and national leaders who have taken the same position on these issues.

Essentially, church leaders were cutting through what Gunnar Myrdal (1963) called the American dilemma—the fact that Americans hold universal values in their creed but live day by day according to particularistic attitudes. Ministers forced members to take into account their more basic values in reacting to specific applications of those values. In many cases, the members' facing up to their own inconsistencies of behavior resulted in their willingness to accept as right some actions that they disliked. Just as every day we perform some obligations that we fully recognize as right yet would prefer not to perform, church members have accepted and even supported policies that they personally disliked and would never have framed by themselves. These results call into question Dean Kelley's (1972) conclusion that churches cannot and should not be agents of social change. Though his emphasis on the meaning-giving function of churches anticipates the core-value approach to legitimacy, he underestimates the extent to which the ultimate values he thinks the church must emphasize can provide leverage for support of social change.

It is important that a claim to legitimacy evoke a voluntary response from those who accept the claim and whose support for the organization's policies is needed. Though Arthur Stinchcombe criticized Weber's emphasis on voluntary compliance as too unstable a basis for leadership, I believe that Weber's insight is crucial for contemporary organizations, especially voluntary organizations. Clearly, leaders of voluntary organizations must elicit an unalienated response, compliance or tolerance or both, from their members. Otherwise, members' dissatisfaction will culminate in exit from the organization. This situation was especially true in a time like the 1970s, when the social atmosphere in general was conducive to challenge of authorities at all levels and in nonvoluntary as well as voluntary organizations; witness the rash of challenges of school attendance policies, dress codes, and so forth. It becomes too cumbersome for officials to be involved continually in litigation, even though the power of the state may be available to enforce their policies.

There is a similarity between the function of legitimacy as I conceive it and the function of loyalty as Albert Hirschman discussed it in his essay *Exit, Voice, and Loyalty* (1970). Loyalty, according to him, neutralizes the tendency of those members who can be most useful to the organization to be the first to exit when they are in disagreement. "As a result of loyalty, these potentially most influential customers and members will stay on longer than they would ordinarily, in the hope or, rather, reasoned expectation that improvement or reform can be received 'from within'" (1970:79).

Though legitimacy could result in loyalty, there is a large difference in our conceptualizations. Hirschman assumed that when the individual disagrees with policy, the organization is wrong and the individual is right. So loyalty causes the individual to stay in the organization, waiting for the organization to change or trying to change it. However, if the organization fails to change, the individual becomes more and more dissatisfied. My understanding of legitimacy suggests the possibility that the organizational policies disagreed with are in fact legitimate policies for the organization. Leaders' activation of a member's belief in legitimacy helps that member to change his or her mind about the acceptability of such policies. This does not necessarily mean that the member's attitude toward the issue will change, though, if the organization is important for the individual, this may be a likely outcome in the long run. Rather, he or she will accept the policies as appropriate, given the organization's values. For Hirschman, then, loyalty holds individuals long enough for them to change the organization or to see whether it will change. In my view, belief in legitimacy holds individuals long enough for reflection on the core values of the organization to change their evaluation of policies.

This theory of legitimacy has not been articulated previously, but it is congruent with previous theories about organizations. For instance, Weber (1968) anticipated a theory of legitimacy based on values. In discussing the bases on which actors ascribe legitimacy to a social order, he listed the three elements from which he generated his pure types of authority (see Chapter 1). In addition, he cited value-rational faith, based on that which has been deduced as an absolute, and gave natural law as an example. Weber did not develop a type of authority based on value-rational faith, and until recently this concept has been entirely neglected by subsequent theorists.[4]

David Willer (1967), however, builds a fourth type of authority on Weber's value-rational basis. According to him, "Ideological authority rests on faith in the absolute value of a ra-

---

4. Michael Hill (1973) interprets Weber's *traditional* basis of legitimacy dynamically, achieving a result similar to that of value-rational faith. Tradition provides normative content for commands, which in turn provides leverage for social change—to "restore" the original character of the organization or of society. In this connection also see Peter Berger (1963).

tionalized set of norms" (1967 : 236). Obedience is not owed to a person; "the content of the commands is legitimated by its relation to the ends of the ideology" (1967 : 236). Leaders hold their positions by virtue of their ability to further the organization's values.[5]

For Chester Barnard (1966) and Philip Selznick (1957), the key role of the leader is to foster the organization's values in a context where many values are competing. According to Barnard, the individuals who are subject to authority determine whether it is authoritative for them. Thus, authority is very fragile. Leaders' "ineptness, ignorance of conditions, failure to communicate what ought to be said" (1966 : 174) can quickly erode it. One way that executives can maintain authority is by managing the incentive system so that individuals' benefits from the organization outweigh the burdens imposed. The collective goals of the organization are relevant in at least two ways: progress toward the collective goals represents for some participants a primary source of individual satisfaction; and collective goals are a basis for an appeal to transcend individual motives. Thus, Barnard concludes, "The inculcation of belief in

5. Willer assumed that value-rational, or ideological, authority would find expression in a bureaucratic structure. In developing Willer's expansion of Weber, however, Roberta Satow (1975) contends that an independent type of organization evolves from the value-rational basis of legitimacy. In this new type of structure, members who are motivated by strongly held ideological beliefs are segmented from those who are not. According to Satow, churches and other organizations in which professionals play a central role are of this type. She points out that during the social movements of the 1960s outspoken religious professionals were on college campuses or in denominational offices where they were not directly vulnerable to members who opposed their pronouncements. She thinks that such segmented structures are the logical solution where groups of persons within an organization are committed to preserving what they perceive to be the organization's ideology. However, as we have seen, segmentation is not possible in the local church context (but see Hadden and Longino, 1974, for an experiment setting up special congregations for social action). Members' resources are needed, and the use of those resources is visible. Therefore, those committing the resources are vulnerable. In this context the ideologue must try to convert others or to resuscitate the ideology within them. Value-rational faith as a basis of legitimacy is important precisely because of its usefulness where segmentation is not possible or where it breaks down.

the real existence of a common purpose is an essential executive function" (1966:87). The executive secures, creates, and inspires morale in an organization by "inculcating points of view, fundamental attitudes, loyalties, to the organizational cooperative system, and to the system of objective authority, that will result in subordinating individual interests and the minor dictates of personal codes, to the good of the cooperative whole" (1966:279). Also, the executive must justify any change or new specification of purpose so that the "sense of conformance to moral codes is secured" (1966:280).

For Selznick (1957), the primary leadership functions are: defining the organization's mission and role; embodying that mission in effective social structures; and defending the organization's distinctive values despite challenges from the outside environment or subgroups within the organization itself. The leader is "primarily an expert in the promotion and protection of values" (1957:28). He is aware that human beings bring all of themselves into the organization and not just the part that is most relevant to its purposes (1957:8). Thus, values outside the organization compete for members' loyalty. Protected enclaves may be used initially to foster precarious values or reinterpretations, but the values should ultimately infuse every facet of the organization. Ideologies that support central values can be used for "boosting internal morale, communicating the bases of decisions, and rebuffing outside claims and criticisms" (1957:14).

Both Barnard and Selznick believed that a principal function of leaders is to implement an organization's core values, and both realized that this function is often resisted by members because they have value attachments outside the organization. However, neither gave much attention to whether members' prior attachment to the core values is genuine. Barnard expected the organization's code to be low in the individual's hierarchy of values and did not discuss how to change this fact. In Selznick's discussion of values and purpose it is not always evident that he refers to collective values, even though he at first links leadership with the determination of public interest. In other words, these theorists seem to envision use of members' resources in support of values that those members have never espoused.

Thus, although it is congruent with the theories of Barnard and Selznick, my theory has a different emphasis: the values that leaders foster are a part of their mandate. Although members may not act on these values unless their consciousness has been raised, the values are part of their value repertoire, and, when reminded, members generally acknowledge the centrality of the values to the organization.

### Applying the Theory
### to Nonchurch Organizations

Churches were a logical starting point for developing a core-value theory of legitimacy because of the historically prominent role of sacred scriptures in church leadership. Roy Rappaport (1971), using the term *sacred* to refer to "the quality of unquestionable truthfulness imputed by the faithful to unverifiable propositions," asserts that human "organization could not have come into existence, or persisted, in the absence of ultimate sacred propositions and the sanctification of discourse" (1971:29). Sanctity has played a predominant role in containing the self-interested pursuits of individuals and social groups and thereby has supported the conventions of the larger society. Associating statements about economic arrangements, political authorities, or other social policies with the ultimate sacred propositions, through ritual or in discursive structures such as theology, "presents to the individual as his own goals those of the society and thus replaces possible recalcitrance with compliance" (1971:39).

Rappaport thus sees at work in the development of societies the sort of legitimating process that I have found in churches. In the church, however, the process is still anchored in a belief in a transcendent being. The question therefore arises whether the core-value theory of legitimacy applies to nonchurch organizations. Of course, a number of nonchurch organizations draw doctrine and ritual from the churches. For example, the core-value theory should certainly apply to the many fraternal organizations that base their rituals directly on the Bible. More important, even nonbelievers in our society are subject to public rituals that affirm sacred principles from the Judaic-Christian tradition. For example, most public officials continue to take an oath of office couched in the terms of that tradition. If Rappaport is correct in asserting that it is "the visible, explicit, public act of acceptance, and not the invisible, ambiguous, private sentiment that is socially and morally binding" (1979:195), then continued exposure to these public rituals may provide a basis on which even leaders in secular organizations can make value appeals. Furthermore, as I shall illustrate by the case of the American Civil Liberties Union (ACLU), the traditions of the Enlightenment and various humanistic philosophies—especially those embodied in the Declaration of Independence, the federal Constitution, and other public documents—enunciate values that can serve as bases of legitimacy in secular organizations in our society. These facts, together with the core-value theory's congruence with general theories of organizations, suggest its wider application. I have already hinted at such applications. Now some illustrations are in order.

The ACLU's defense in 1978 of a nazi organization's right to hold a rally in Skokie, Illinois, provides a prime example of a nonchurch organization implementing a value-based decision despite a severe threat to that organization's ability to maintain itself. The case was intensely emotional because of the presence in Skokie of a large number of concentration camp survivors. Thousands of ACLU members resigned, and income dropped so severely that a layoff of office staff became necessary. During this crisis David Goldberger, the ACLU lawyer who argued the Skokie case, authored a widely circulated appeal for support for his organization. The appeal was cast in terms of the central values of the ACLU and mentioned "freedom of speech," "the First Amendment," "the Bill of Rights," "civil liberties," "important human values," and "human rights." The heart of the appeal was a distinction between personal attitudes toward a nazi rally and belief in the fundamental values championed by the ACLU: "The nazis asked us to defend their right to hold the rally, and to challenge one of the laws prohibiting it. Though I detested their beliefs, I went into court to defend the First Amendment."

My second illustration is a hypothetical one. Imagine a local chapter of the National Association for the Advancement of Colored People that was organized by a group of people primarily concerned to achieve a specific objective, such as the integration of motels and restaurants in their community. If the chapter continues long beyond the achievement of that objective without facing a controversial issue, it is likely that most members would be deriving mainly solidary benefits from the organization.[6] When new areas of controversy arise—for example, the integration of schools—many such members might oppose the organization's involvement. Yet leaders would betray their mandate if they simply gave in to the opposition of such members. The theory of core-value legitimacy suggests the strategy of raising members' consciousness of the basic values of the organization and of the relation between those values and the specific issue the organization has tackled.

Professions and professional organizations also foster secular values that can legitimate actions that are not always popular. Robert Merton, George Reader, and Patricia Kendall (1957) pointed out the need for leaders in medicine to appeal to the major values of medicine in order to legitimate resistance to demands from particular groups in society and also to instill in graduates of medical schools the norms that will insulate them from society's pressures, such as for popular but useless treatments. If the medical profession were to join particular battles against unhealthy aspects of the environment, such as industrial pollution or unsafe automobiles, the most appropriate strat-

6. Peter Clark and James Wilson (1961) argue that organizations are likely to emphasize goals as incentives when they are new but that as they grow older, they are more likely to offer material incentives—for example, business contacts—or solidary incentives, such as prestige, fun, and fellowship.

egy for leaders seeking support from the profession, as well as from the community, would be to appeal to the core values of the profession itself.

Tying these examples together are the attempts of the leaders of each organization to gain the support of members and potential members by causing them to look at particular issues in the light of values central to the organization. Of course, the success of any appeal to core values may well depend on the organization's previous attention to socialization of members.

Obviously, the context in which leaders must make such decisions is far more complex than these few illustrations can suggest. For example, members' resistance to policies that leaders claim are based on core values may itself be based on core values, with members arguing that the leaders' policies are in fact contradictory to those values. The rich complexity of the subject invites future research.

## Legitimacy and National Leaders

Rappaport contends that the increasing coercive power of central authorities has made their reliance on sanctification less necessary. More important, I think, is the increasing diversity of society, which makes reliance on sanctification less possible at the national level. Less than fifteen years ago Robert Bellah (1967) could still make a convincing case for the existence of an American civil religion that provided religious legitimation for the presidency. This civil religion allowed a religious dimension to the political realm while relegating loyalty to particular churches and specific religious doctrines to the private sphere. During 1980 that arrangement was under heavy attack by such large, well-funded groups as the Moral Majority and Christian Voice. These groups appeared determined to make their specific Christian doctrines a test for entrance to political office (see Mayer et al., 1980; Thomas, 1980).[7]

7. Liberal religious groups have also threatened civil religion arrangements in the past, for example, at the height of the civil rights movement. The present threat seems more ominous because the conservatives are far more numerous

The most extensive and most impressive development of a value theory of leadership at the national level is James Burns's (1978) wide-ranging essay on leadership. Burns, however, may not fully appreciate the implications of the diversity of value orientations in modern societies. He defines leadership as "leaders inducing followers to act for certain goals that represent the values and the motivations . . . *of both leaders and followers.*" Apparently, he envisions national leaders appealing directly to the populace for allegiance. For example, he sees Mao Tse-tung as a classic leader, one who not only comprehended the existing needs of his followers but also mobilized "within them newer motivations and aspirations that would in the future furnish a popular foundation for the kind of leadership Mao hoped to supply" (1978 : 254).

My understanding of core-value legitimacy implies a different interpretation of national leadership, at least as applied to contemporary American society. First, our society is too diverse for any clear consensus on the core values of the nation. Amid such diversity it seems that national leaders would achieve their greatest effectiveness in forging consensus by working with the multitude of organized collectivities rather than by making direct appeals to individual citizens. The effect of direct appeals on individual citizens is, as Amitai Etzioni (1968 : 433) says, largely determined not by their specific nature or by the leaders who make them but by the citizens' multiple memberships in groups and organizations. Hence, though my theory is in many respects compatible with Burns's, I am much less sanguine than he appears to be about the direct application of value theory to the relationship between contemporary national leaders and individual citizens. I believe the major potential contribution that my study of churches can make to an understanding of this broader context for leadership is in describing how multiple organizational memberships can affect members'

---

than the liberals, and they control a vast network of radio and television communications. On the other hand, it is impossible to tell how well and how long the various elements of the conservative coalition can be held together.

attitudes toward one organization's policies and what conditions will allow the influence of some memberships to outweigh that of others.

The second problem I see with Burns's application of value theory to national units is his failure to specify the social grounding of values. The "newer motivations" mobilized by a leader such as Mao or Hitler might very well be destructive to the society as a whole. The original association of values with the sacred is predicated on the existence of a transcendent being, but in the absence of such a belief the grounding of values in tradition or in pluralistic compromise offers protection against the misguided leader with an idiosyncratic notion of what the society's values should be. If a society is too diverse to have a widely agreed upon set of core values, then it appears that national leaders must forge policy in cooperation with leaders of those organizations that are the repositories of the various values within the nation. Core-value legitimacy can give leaders within these organizations a basis for checking a too facile allegiance to charismatic national leaders (Kornhauser, 1959) and for mobilizing their members against oligarchical rule by any faction of society.

## Conclusion

Undeniably, as Michels observed, some structural constraints encourage organizational leaders to be conservative. However, other structural constraints can encourage liberal attitudes and policies (Zald and Ash, 1966). The latter include relationships to leaders in other organizations, as in coalitions (Wood, 1975), and to leaders in the community in general (Stouffer, 1963). Moreover, an organization that has altruistic, universalistic, or other liberal values makes its leaders conscious that they are charged with fostering those values. In fact, an organization may be most effective in fostering values among its members when its leaders have or develop a vested interest in the organization's core values (Selznick, 1957).

Leadership is often demanding enough that even a high salary cannot induce the devotion needed from leaders.

Further development of the theory of legitimacy based on collective values would not only counter the more pessimistic view that is the legacy of Michels but also provide a way out of Michels's dilemma. He saw no real hope for the achievement of collective goals outside of organizations but was convinced that organization inevitably leads to displacement of these goals by leaders' personal goals. He assumed that majority will should be the only guide to leaders' behavior and that it was the only means by which leaders could establish the legitimacy of their actions. Yet many organizations exist precisely to foster values that are precarious when left to individuals. According to my theory, the leaders of these organizations should base their claim to leadership on their loyalty to those values. This view does not preclude the possibility that leaders will pursue their own selfish interests with organizational resources. Theoretically, though, leaders are no more likely to follow this pattern of behavior than are members, because of their participation in other value-giving social networks, likely to attempt to pull the organization toward other values, causing value displacement. There is even good reason, theoretically, to believe that the latter is more likely to occur, because the organization usually is a more salient value community for leaders than for the average member.

Michels failed to consider that organizations are not simply collections of individuals but also structural entities that act within a context of certain freedoms and constraints. We should not ignore the dangers of oligarchy, but neither should we ignore the fundamental importance of organizations that hold individuals to their more universal values when their particularistic values are pulling them in other directions (Olson, 1968). Much of the ferment in the churches over social action has resulted from attempts to lead the collectivity in accordance with the basic values that members learn in the church rather than with the attitudes they derive from other networks of social interaction (for example, work groups, country clubs). The present study testifies that these attempts are sometimes successful.

The fundamental empirical question about the legitimacy of leadership is not whether transcendence of members' attitudes has occurred but whether that transcendence is in the direction of the organization's core values. If so, the burden of proof is on those who want to accuse leaders of oligarchy in a pejorative sense, and the proper assumption is that leaders have claimed legitimacy on the basis of their belief in the organization's values and have had that claim honored by the membership. The point, of course, is not to assess transcendence as morally good or bad—the values of some organizations may be immoral from the point of view of others—but to understand it as a sociological reality. Without such social mechanisms, individuals could hardly become social units, and the values best fostered in and by such units would vanish. This insight is not the exclusive property of sociology or of the political liberal. A contemporary political commentator, writing about the state, captured it precisely:

> The state is more than a device for serving the immediate preferences of its citizens. Its purpose is to achieve collective objectives. . . . Thus the state's legitimate purposes are more complex than the sum of the citizens' private purposes; the public interest is not just the automatic, unguided outcome of the maelstrom of private interests (Will, 1976).

# Appendix A
# Methodology

## Sampling Details

I selected seven Protestant denominations that had the following characteristics: at least one million members nationally; a fairly large number of churches in the Indianapolis area; and a history of active participation in social issues. The denominations included in the study were: the American Baptist Churches in the U.S.A.; the Christian Church (Disciples of Christ); the Lutheran Church in America; the Protestant Episcopal Church; the United Church of Christ; The United Methodist Church; and The United Presbyterian Church in the United States of America. These denominations offered a diversity of formal control structures.

Indianapolis (Marion County) churches of these denominations were systematically selected according to a plan designed by Irene Hess of the Institute of Social Research, University of Michigan. First, the 11 largest churches were selected with certainty. These churches ranged in size from 1,737 to 3,072 members, with an average of 2,003 members. The remaining churches were then selected randomly after having been stratified by denomination and, within each denomination, arranged in order of size. The number of local churches selected from each denomination was proportional to the number of members of that denomination in Indianapolis. This technique has the advantage of allowing either organizations or individuals to be treated as the unit of analysis. However, when individuals were the unit of analysis, it was necessary to weight respondents in each church by a fraction representing that church's proportion of the total target population divided by the proportion of the total sample in that church.

Of the 60 churches that were chosen initially, 52 met our criteria for selection, and 40 (77 percent) of those agreed to participate. (In addition to criteria already mentioned, we sampled only churches that had traditionally had a predominately white membership, and we excluded those churches whose current minister had served less than one year.) The 12 churches that refused to participate were replaced by churches that had been designated as replacements by the original sampling procedure (they were of the same denomination and as similar in size to the original churches as possible). Later, because of special interest in the mixed polity of Lutheranism, 2 more Lutheran churches were added for a total of 4. The final sample of churches included 22 Methodist, 10 Christian, 8 Presbyterian, 7 Baptist, 4 Lutheran, 4 United Church of Christ, and 3 Episcopal churches.

Seventy-five members per church were randomly selected from a list that each church had prepared of members who were at least 18 years old, who lived in the Indianapolis area, and who had participated in the local church by attending or making a contribution within the two years preceding the mailing of questionnaires in October 1973. However, the 11 largest churches were sampled at the rate of one selection for each 23 members.

After two follow-up mailings, 2,165 members had returned usable questionnaires, a response rate of 54 percent. The principal lay officers of each church (the number varied by polity) received officer questionnaires. Of the officers, 204 (57 percent) returned usable questionnaires. Information on nonrespondents came from ministers and from a telephone survey of 96 randomly chosen nonrespondents.

Nonrespondents' age distribution did not differ significantly from that of respondents, but males (43 percent of the nonrespondents but only 36 percent of the respondents) and infrequent church attenders were relatively unlikely to respond to the survey. Weekly church attendance was reported by 57.2 percent of the respondents and 41 percent of the nonrespondents; 22.4 percent of the respondents, but 38 percent of the nonrespondents, reported attending only monthly or less often. The occupational distributions of respondents and nonrespondents were quite similar. However, clerical workers and professionals were somewhat overrepresented among respondents, and homemakers were somewhat underrepresented. Almost identical percentages of respondents and resurveyed nonrespondents (73.4 percent and 74 percent, respectively) agreed that they were proud that their denomination speaks out on social issues. However, 18 percent of the nonrespondents, but only 9.3 percent of the respondents, declined to express an opinion on denominational action.

The possible nonresponse bias that gave us most concern derived from the overrepresentation of females and frequent church attenders among the respondents. In order to minimize the possible bias, we weighted the respondents. Within each church, I assigned each respondent to one of four sex-attendance categories: male frequent attenders, that is, attendance at least once a week; female frequent attenders; male infrequent attenders; and female infrequent attenders. (Estimates of attendance of nonrespondents were usually supplied by the minister, but some churches kept attendance records.) I assigned each respondent a weight equal to the total N of the category divided by the respondent N of that category. When churches rather than members are the units of analysis, member means or medians are employed as church properties and are derived from weighted data.

Significance tests are based on a random model, even though the member sample is technically a mixture of simple random and random samples within clusters. Though weighting procedures reduced the N of respondents from 2,165 to a weighted N of 1,747, thus compensating somewhat for the loss of efficiency resulting from clustering, the significance levels involving members are best interpreted cautiously. Hence, even though the study is somewhat exploratory, the levels reported are .001, .01, and .05.

## Measures

The measures used in the statistical analyses but not fully described in the text are here presented in the order of their appearance in the book. See Appendix B for the entire membership questionnaire.

CHAPTER 2

*Attitudes toward welfare.* Members' and ministers' attitudes toward welfare were compared on the following scale:

> In American society, any individual with ability and ambition can earn a good income.
> We are spending too *little* money on welfare programs in this country.
> I would support my minister if he were [minister form: It is proper for a minister] to participate in a picket line or demonstration on behalf of underprivileged people.

Response choices for these three items were: strongly agree; agree; disagree; strongly disagree.

> How would you respond if your local church or its leaders took these actions:
>> Provided space in the church for meetings of welfare mothers seeking to challenge rulings of public welfare agencies.
>> Contributed funds to a welfare rights organization.

Choices for these two items were: I would strongly approve; I would approve; I would disapprove; I would strongly disapprove.

The reliability of the scale is indicated by a Cronbach's Alpha of .71.

*Attitudes toward racial justice.* The following scale was administered to both ministers and members:

How would you respond if your local church or its leaders took these actions:

> Provided space in the church for meetings of the local chapter of the National Association for the Advancement of Colored People.
>
> Contributed money to a minority group in response to the demand that churches pay reparations for their part in discrimination against that group.
>
> Held a marriage ceremony for an interracial couple.

Response choices were: strongly agree; agree; disagree; and strongly disagree.

> My denomination should censure local churches which refuse to accept black members.
>
> Churches should refuse to do business with firms unwilling to hire blacks on the same basis as whites.
>
> American churches should provide money for the economic advancement of black Americans.

Response choices for these three items were: I would strongly approve; I would approve; I would disapprove; I would strongly disapprove.

Cronbach's Alpha for the scale is .72.

CHAPTER 3

*Education.* See item 202 in the questionnaire.

*Age.* See item 197 in the questionnaire.

*Income.* See item 200 in the questionnaire.

*Occupation.* See item 201 in the questionnaire.

*Sex.* See item 198 in the questionnaire.

*Religious beliefs.* Items 18, 19, 20, 21, 22, and 23 composed the well-known religious beliefs scale developed by Charles Glock and Rodney Stark (1966).

*Denominational influence.* One item composed this scale: "My denomination is an important influence on my attitudes toward social issues." Possible answers were: strongly agree; agree; disagree; strongly disagree.

CHAPTER 4

*Formal legitimacy.* This variable is measured as a dichotomy between those denominations in which the local church owns its own property and can hire and fire its own minister and those denominations in which one or both of these rights is formally located at a point in the denominational structure above the local church.

*Belief in legitimacy.* Four items composed this scale. Possible responses were: strongly agree; agree; disagree; strongly disagree.

> It is not right for a local church to disregard the counsel of denominational leaders.
> The denomination's position *should* carry most weight in determining my local church's involvement in social issues.
> Even when I disagree, I feel a moral obligation to support the social policies of my denomination.
> If policies of my local church and denomination were in conflict on some issue, I would feel obligated to follow the denomination's policies.

Cronbach's Alpha for the scale is .70.

CHAPTER 5

*Ministers' belief in legitimacy.* There were 12 items in this scale. The possible reponses were: strongly agree; agree; disagree; strongly disagree.

> The local church (rather than the denomination) is always the best judge of who should be admitted to its membership.
> My first loyalty is to my local church, not to the denomination.
> It is not right for a local church to disregard the counsel of denominational leaders.
> The denomination's position *should* carry most weight in determining my local church's involvement in social issues.
> My denomination is an important influence on my attitudes toward social issues.
> I want my local church to be closely tied with the denomination.
> On social action issues, each local church should make its own decisions.
> I wish my local church were not so much under the influence of the denomination.

I would be distressed if my local church were to withdraw from the denomination.

Even when I disagree, I feel a moral obligation to support the social policies of my denomination.

Denominational leaders should respect the right of local churches to make their own decisions no matter what the issue.

If policies of my local church and denomination were in conflict on some issue, I would feel obligated to follow the denomination's policies.

Cronbach's Alpha for this scale is .88.

*Tolerance of dissonant policy.* This scale is based on 16 two-stage questions (see items 52, 53, 54, 55, 57, 58, 59, 60, 61, 62, 64, 65, 67, 68, 69, and 70 in the questionnaire) in which respondents were first asked to indicate their approval or disapproval of hypothetical actions by their local church and then, if they disapproved, were asked to indicate "the *strongest* expression of disapproval" they would be willing to make.

Each item was scored according to the following scale of tolerance: 1 = least tolerant; 5 = most tolerant. Then scores for the several items were added together to obtain total scores on the tolerance of dissonant policy scale.

| | |
|---|---|
| Attempt to have the minister dismissed | 1 |
| Join another local church | 1 |
| Stay away from church services | 2 |
| Withhold donations and pledges | 2 |
| Enlist the support of other members | 3 |
| Write a letter of protest to local officer | 3 |
| Write a letter of protest to denominational officer | 3 |
| Bring the matter before the official board | 3 |
| Discuss the matter with the minister | 4 |
| Would *not* openly express disapproval | 5 |

Cronbach's Alpha for this scale is .95.

*Apathy.* This eight-item scale had a Cronbach's Alpha of .73.

I often wonder why I go to church at all.

Religious beliefs influence all my dealings in life.

I feel there are many more important things in life than religion.

People like me don't have any say about what the church does.

The central interests of my life are not closely related to the church.

To be perfectly honest, I don't care what my local church says or does about social issues.

Possible responses for these six items were: strongly agree; agree; disagree; strongly disagree. The remaining two items were:

Do you read denominational literature frequently, occasionally, rarely or never?

How often do you attend worship services of your *local church?* (Possible answers: twice a week or more; once a week; 2–3 times a month; once a month; less often.)

# Appendix B
## The Membership Questionnaire

CHURCH PARTICIPATION SURVEY

Ballantine Hall 744
Indiana University
Bloomington, Indiana 47401

We are interested in knowing more about church people in Indianapolis—how *you* participate in your church and community and *your* opinions about several issues that are much discussed by the public today.

Please read the following instructions before you begin.

*Instructions*

1. Please do *not* put your name on the questionnaire as we want to guarantee that every individual's responses are held in strictest confidence.

2. Please answer *every* question (unless the directions say that a certain question is not for you).

3. When answering questions with a limited number of choices, please choose the answer that comes *closest* to the right answer for you, even if it does not fit perfectly. (*After* you have marked the closest answer, you may write a qualification in the margin if you like.)

4. Most questions can be answered simply by putting a circle around the number following the answer which comes closest to the right answer for you. For example:

Do you have a job?

Yes ............................ ①  [23]
No ............................ 2

These code numbers are necessary for processing the answers you and others give to the questions.
*All* numbers in brackets (such as [23] above) are also for our use in data processing and should be ignored.

5. Religious groups may differ in their use of some terms. We will use *"Local church"* to mean the church where you attend services. By *"denomination"* we mean the national body with which your local church is affiliated. *"Official board"* will mean the principal governing or coordinating body of your local church.

6. When you have finished the questionnaire, please mail it back to us in the enclosed postage-paid envelope. At the same time, please also mail back the post card attached to your questionnaire as it is very important that we know when you have responded.

Thank you very much for your cooperation; we hope you enjoy filling out this questionnaire.

*111*

[731...........................01]

I. First of all, we would like some information about your religious background and church activity.

1. Please circle the number following the *denomination* to which you belong.

American Baptist Churches, USA .............. 1    [10]
Christian Church (Disciples) ...................... 2
Lutheran Church in America ...................... 3
Protestant Episcopal Church ...................... 4
United Church of Christ ............................ 5
The United Methodist Church .................. 6
United Presbyterian Church, USA ............ 7
Other (please specify) .............................. 8

2. Please print here the name of the local church to which you presently belong.
Name of local church                        [11-12]

3. How long have you been a member of your present local church? Please circle the answer which is closest.

Less than 1 year ...................................... 1    [13]
1 to 2 years ............................................ 2
3 to 5 years ............................................ 3
6 to 10 years .......................................... 4
More than 10 years (but not *always*) ......... 5
I have *always* been a member (since I
was old enough) .................................... 6

4. Have you ever been a member of a denomination other than your present one?

Yes ........................................................ 1    [14]
No ......................................................... 2

IF YES
4a. What denomination was that? (If more than one, list them in order from the most recent to the earliest. Please give *full title* if you can.)
1. ...................................................... [15-16]
2. ...................................................... [17-18]
3. ...................................................... [19-20]
4. ...................................................... [21-22]

4b. What was your reason for changing to this present *denomination?* Circle the most important reason.

Marriage ................................................ 1    [23]
Because of relatives or friends ................ 2
Dissatisfaction with previous denomination's
social action policies .............................. 3
Liked ritual, liturgy, mode of worship,
etc. of present denomination .................. 4
Proximity of location .............................. 5
Emphasis on education ............................ 6
Community involvement .......................... 7
Theological reasons ................................ 8

5. If you have children, *or* if you ever were to have children, how important would it be to you that your children stay in your *denomination?*

Very important ...................................... 1    [24]
Important ............................................. 2
Not very important ................................ 3
Not important at all ................................ 4

6. What was your mother's denominational **affiliation** when you were living at home?

Same as *my* present denomination .............. 1  [25-26]
Other (please give full title if you can)
.............................................................. 2

7. What was your father's denominational **affiliation** when you were living at home?

Same as *my* present denomination .............. 1  [27-28]
Other (please give full title if you can)
.............................................................. 2

IF YOU ARE PRESENTLY MARRIED

8. What is your spouse's present denominational affiliation?
Same as *my* present denomination ............... 1  [29-30]
Other (please give full title if you can)
.............................................................. 2

9. How often do you attend worship services of your *local church?*

Twice a week or more ............................ 1    [31]
Once a week .......................................... 2
2-3 times a month .................................. 3
Once a month ........................................ 4
Less often ............................................. 5

10. How long does it take you to drive to Sunday services?

Less than 10 minutes .............................. 1    [32]
10-20 minutes ........................................ 2
20-30 minutes ........................................ 3
30-45 minutes ........................................ 4
More than 45 minutes ............................ 5

11. About how much money did you give to your local church in the past year?

None ..................................................01   [33-34]
Less than $50 ......................................02
$50 to $99 ..........................................03
$100 to $199 ......................................04
$200 to $399 ......................................05
$400 to $599 ......................................06
$600 to $999 ......................................07
$1,000 to $1,999 ................................08
$2,000 to $2,999 ................................09
$3,000 or more ..................................10

12. Do you belong to any organizations or groups in your *local church?*

Yes ...................................................... 1    [35]
No ....................................................... 2

IF YES
12a. About how many hours do you devote to this (these) group(s) in an average month?

Less than an hour .................................. 1    [36]
One hour ............................................... 2
Two hours ............................................ 3
Three hours .......................................... 4
Four hours ............................................ 5
Five hours ............................................ 6
More than five hours ............................ 7

13. Do you hold or have you recently held any office in your *local church* (or in one of these groups)?

Yes ...................................................... 1    [37]
No ....................................................... 2

14. Think for a moment of your five closest friends; how many are members of your *local church?*

None ..................................................... 1    [38]
One ....................................................... 2
Two ....................................................... 3
Three .................................................... 4
Four ...................................................... 5
Five ...................................................... 6

15. In the last year, how many conversations (*not* just greetings at the church door) have you had with your minister?

None ..................................................... 1    [39]
One ....................................................... 2
Two or three .......................................... 3
Four or five ........................................... 4
More than five ....................................... 5

16. Compared to the average member's participation in your local church, would you say that you participate more, less, or about the same?

| | | |
|---|---|---|
| More | 1 | [40] |
| Less | 2 | |
| About like the average | 3 | |

17. Has your participation in your local church increased, decreased, or remained about the same in the last few years?

| | | |
|---|---|---|
| Increased | 1 | [41] |
| Decreased | 2 | |
| Remained about the same | 3 | |

IF YOUR PARTICIPATION HAS INCREASED

17a. Circle the number after the most important reason.

| | | |
|---|---|---|
| More time available | 1 | [42] |
| Better health | 2 | |
| Stronger personal faith | 3 | |
| Accepted office or other responsibility in the church | 4 | |
| Because of the children | 5 | |
| More positive attitude toward the local church and/or denomination | 6 | |

IF YOUR PARTICIPATION HAS DECREASED

17b. Circle the number after the most important reason.

| | | |
|---|---|---|
| Less time available | 1 | [43] |
| Health problems | 2 | |
| Decreased personal faith | 3 | |
| Gave up an office or other responsibility in the church | 4 | |
| The children are now less involved | 5 | |
| More negative attitude toward the local church and/or denomination | 6 | |

II. These next questions are about your religious beliefs and worship experiences.

18. Which of the following statements comes closest to what you believe about God?

| | | |
|---|---|---|
| I know God really exists and I have no doubts about it | 1 | [44] |
| While I have doubts, I feel that I do believe in God | 2 | |
| I find myself believing in God some of the time, but not at other times | 3 | |
| I don't believe in a personal God, but I do believe in a higher power of some kind | 4 | |
| I don't know whether there is a God, and I don't believe there is any way to find out | 5 | |

19. Which of the following statements comes closest to what you believe about Jesus?

| | | |
|---|---|---|
| Jesus is the Divine Son of God and I have no doubts about it | 1 | [45] |
| While I have some doubts, I feel basically that Jesus is Divine | 2 | |
| I feel that Jesus was a great man and very holy, but I don't feel Him to be the Son of God any more than all of us are children of God | 3 | |
| I think Jesus was only a man, although an extraordinary one | 4 | |
| Frankly, I'm not entirely sure there was such a person as Jesus | 5 | |

How do you feel about each of these statements?

20. "There is a life beyond death."

| | | |
|---|---|---|
| Completely true | 1 | [46] |
| Probably true | 2 | |
| Probably not true | 3 | |
| Definitely not true | 4 | |

21. "The Devil actually exists."

| | | |
|---|---|---|
| Completely true | 1 | [47] |
| Probably true | 2 | |
| Probably not true | 3 | |
| Definitely not true | 4 | |

22. "God answers prayer."

| | | |
|---|---|---|
| Completely true | 1 | [48] |
| Probably true | 2 | |
| Probably not true | 3 | |
| Definitely not true | 4 | |

23. "I believe in the Virgin birth of Jesus."

| | | |
|---|---|---|
| Strongly agree | 1 | [49] |
| Agree | 2 | |
| Disagree | 3 | |
| Strongly disagree | 4 | |

24. "Innovations in worship, such as music played on guitars, should be encouraged."

| | | |
|---|---|---|
| Strongly agree | 1 | [50] |
| Agree | 2 | |
| Disagree | 3 | |
| Strongly disagree | 4 | |

25. "I often wonder why I go to church at all."

| | | |
|---|---|---|
| Strongly agree | 1 | [51] |
| Agree | 2 | |
| Disagree | 3 | |
| Strongly disagree | 4 | |

26. "Churches today stress efficient business operation more than spiritual and moral guidance."

| | | |
|---|---|---|
| Strongly agree | 1 | [52] |
| Agree | 2 | |
| Disagree | 3 | |
| Strongly disagree | 4 | |

27. "What religion offers me most is comfort when sorrows and misfortune strike."

| | | |
|---|---|---|
| Strongly agree | 1 | [53] |
| Agree | 2 | |
| Disagree | 3 | |
| Strongly disagree | 4 | |

28. "Religious beliefs influence all my dealings in life."

| | | |
|---|---|---|
| Strongly agree | 1 | [54] |
| Agree | 2 | |
| Disagree | 3 | |
| Strongly disagree | 4 | |

29. "It is important to me to spend periods of time in private religious thought and meditation."

| | | |
|---|---|---|
| Strongly agree | 1 | [55] |
| Agree | 2 | |
| Disagree | 3 | |
| Strongly disagree | 4 | |

30. "I feel there are many more important things in life than religion."

| | | |
|---|---|---|
| Strongly agree | 1 | [56] |
| Agree | 2 | |
| Disagree | 3 | |
| Strongly disagree | 4 | |

III. Now we want to know how you feel about participation in the church generally and in your local church in particular.

31. Listed below are several reasons often given by people when they are asked why they participate in the church. After reading the list carefully, please indicate the three reasons you feel are *most important* for your own participation in your local church.

Enter here the number in front of the *one* reason which *best* explains your church participation ..................——— [57-58]

Enter here the number in front of the reason which is *second* in importance in your own participation ..................——— [59-60]

Enter here the number in front of the reason which is *third* in importance in your own participation ..................——— [61-62]

01 The church gives me a means of helping those in need (such as the sick, aged, lonely, or bereaved).

02 It's the expected thing to do in our community.

03 Many church activities are just plain fun.

04 I participate out of force of habit.

05 It's good for business.

06 It's a good way to meet people.

07 It's the best way to serve God.

08 My spouse wants me to participate.

09 It is a way of exerting influence on the community to provide opportunity and justice for all citizens.

10 It is a basis for knowing God's will for my life.

11 The church gives me an opportunity to help young people.

12 The church gives me a means of contributing to the solution of social problems.

13 My friends want me to participate.

14 Church participation helps me to feel close to God.

15 It gives me a chance to associate with the most influential people in the community.

16 My parents want me to participate.

17 I attend church for intellectual stimulation.

18 It helps train my children in religious values.

19 It helps me find answers to the basic relationships between myself and others.

[731..............................02]

32. What *single* thing do you like best about your *local church*?

| | |
|---|---|
| Its conservative theology .............................. | 01 [10-11] |
| Its liberal theology ..................... | 02 |
| Its friendliness ............................. | 03 |
| Informality of worship .................... | 04 |
| Formality of worship ..................... | 05 |
| Its concern with saving souls ......... | 06 |
| Involvement in social action ....... | 07 |
| Youth ministry and church school ......... | 08 |
| Its concern with human need ........ | 09 |
| Its democratic atmosphere ......... | 10 |
| Its strong leadership ................ | 11 |

33. As your local church draws up its next budget, what priority would you like given to the following activities?

Enter here the number in front of the activity you would like to have *first* priority .........................——— [12]

Enter here the number in front of the activity you would like to have *second* priority .........................——— [13]

Enter here the number in front of the activity you would like to have *third* priority .........................——— [14]

1 Church administration
2 World missions
3 National missions
4 Evangelism
5 Education
6 Social action concerns
7 Disaster relief
8 Fellowship and recreation activities

IV. In this section we are interested in the way you personally participate in making decisions in your local church. We also want to know your impressions of how others participate in the decision-making process.

34. People have different ideas of how they, themselves, fit into church affairs. How would you say you fit into your local church?
Are you:

| | | |
|---|---|---|
| A person who contributes to church decisions ............................................ | 1 | [15] |
| A person who is active, but not one of the decision makers ............................................ | 2 | |
| Just an ordinary church member .................. | 3 | |
| Not really part of this church at all ........... | 4 | |

35. How often do you give information (facts and ideas) concerning local church matters to the *following persons?* (Consider in your answer the information which you give through discussions, at meetings, in private, by letter and telephone.)
Your minister:

| | | |
|---|---|---|
| Never ................................................ | 1 | [16] |
| About once a year ......................... | 2 | |
| A few times a year ........................ | 3 | |
| Once or twice a month .................. | 4 | |
| Several times a month or more often ........... | 5 | |

Members of the official board:

| | | |
|---|---|---|
| Never ................................................ | 1 | [17] |
| About once a year ......................... | 2 | |
| A few times a year ........................ | 3 | |
| Once or twice a month .................. | 4 | |
| Several times a month or more often ........... | 5 | |

Other members of the local church:

| | | |
|---|---|---|
| Never ................................................ | 1 | [18] |
| About once a year ......................... | 2 | |
| A few times a year ........................ | 3 | |
| Once or twice a month .................. | 4 | |
| Several times a month or more often ........... | 5 | |

36. If you wanted to suggest a change in your local church policies, who do you think would be most helpful in getting it adopted?

| | | |
|---|---|---|
| Minister ................................................ | 1 | [19] |
| Members of official board ..................... | 2 | |
| Powerful members of the congregation who are not on the board ............................. | 3 | |
| Congregation as a whole ..................... | 4 | |
| A specific group (please specify) ................ | 5 | |

37. Think for a moment of the members who contribute to your local church decisions. Could they best be described as:

Individuals who act independently of each
other .......................................................... 1   [20]
Members of a single clique (circle of
friends) ....................................................... 2
Members of several cliques ........................... 3

38. How much influence do the following individuals have in your local church?  (Circle the number under the appropriate answer.)

| | Little or no influence | Some influence | Quite a bit of influence | A great deal of influence | A very great deal of influence | |
|---|---|---|---|---|---|---|
| Minister | 1 | 2 | 3 | 4 | 5 | [21] |
| Members of the board | 1 | 2 | 3 | 4 | 5 | [22] |
| Congregation as a whole | 1 | 2 | 3 | 4 | 5 | [23] |
| Those members with more money | 1 | 2 | 3 | 4 | 5 | [24] |
| Those members with stronger religious beliefs | 1 | 2 | 3 | 4 | 5 | [25] |
| Those members with more education | 1 | 2 | 3 | 4 | 5 | [26] |

39. How much influence *would you like* the following individuals to have in your *local church?*

| | Little or no influence | Some influence | Quite a bit of influence | A great deal of influence | A very great deal of influence | |
|---|---|---|---|---|---|---|
| Minister | 1 | 2 | 3 | 4 | 5 | [27] |
| Members of the board | 1 | 2 | 3 | 4 | 5 | [28] |
| Congregation as a whole | 1 | 2 | 3 | 4 | 5 | [29] |
| Those members with more money | 1 | 2 | 3 | 4 | 5 | [30] |
| Those members with stronger religious beliefs | 1 | 2 | 3 | 4 | 5 | [31] |
| Those members with more education | 1 | 2 | 3 | 4 | **5** | [32] |

40. Some members of this local church have a great deal of influence whether or not they are on the official board.

Strongly agree ............................................. 1   [33]
Agree ........................................................... 2
Disagree ....................................................... 3
Strongly disagree ......................................... 4

41. People like me don't have any say about what the church does.

Strongly agree ............................................. 1   [34]
Agree ........................................................... 2
Disagree ....................................................... 3
Strongly disagree ......................................... 4

42. When I think of my *local church* I usually think in terms of *they* rather than *we.*

Strongly agree ............................................. 1   [35]
Agree ........................................................... 2
Disagree ....................................................... 3
Strongly disagree ......................................... 4

43. Sometimes church policies seem so complicated that I can't really understand what's going on.

Strongly agree ............................................. 1   [36]
Agree ........................................................... 2
Disagree ....................................................... 3
Strongly disagree ......................................... 4

44. Some members of this local church seem to have a lot more influence over policy than others.

Strongly agree ............................................. 1   [37]
Agree ........................................................... 2
Disagree ....................................................... 3
Strongly disagree ......................................... 4

45. Suppose your minister wanted to make a change in your local church's policies and he felt the change might be controversial. He might consider the opinion of several individuals or groups. Please *rank* the following according to their probable ability to influence his decision. Place the number of the most

important influence in the first blank below, the number of the second most important influence in the second blank, and so on.

1  Denominational officials
2  Other ministers
3  Members of the local church official board
4  Certain influential members of the local church whether or not they were on the official board
5  The congregation as a whole
6  The minister's personal opinion regarding the change

       _____ 1      [38]
       _____ 2      [39]
       _____ 3      [40]
       _____ 4      [41]
       _____ 5      [42]
       _____ 6      [43]

46.  To what extent do people in your local church see eye-to-eye on things about the everyday operation (or general policies) of your local church?

Complete agreement ........................... 1    [44]
Fairly complete agreement ................ 2
Fairly complete disagreement' ........... 3
Complete disagreement ...................... 4

47.  How would you describe the relationship between your present minister and the members who most actively contribute to your local church's decisions. Do they appear to agree:

Almost all of the time ................... 1    [45]
Often, but not always ................... 2
Sometimes ................................... 3
Seldom ...................................... 4

*or*  Does the minister appear to be in frequent agreement with some and frequent disagreement with some others ............... 5

48.  How satisfied are you with the progress your local church is making toward fulfilling goals which you consider important?

Very satisfied ............................... 1    [46]
Generally satisfied ........................ 2
Somewhat dissatisfied ................... 3
Very dissatisfied .......................... 4

49.  How satisfied are you with your fellow church members?

Very satisfied ............................... 1    [47]
Generally satisfied ........................ 2
Somewhat dissatisfied ................... 3
Very dissatisfied .......................... 4

50.  How satisfied are you with your minister?

Very satisfied ............................... 1    [48]
Generally satisfied ........................ 2
Somewhat dissatisfied ................... 3
Very dissatisfied .......................... 4

V.  In this section we list a number of actions which local churches might take in relation to community organizations or issues. Please indicate in each case how you would be likely to respond if your local church or its leaders took these actions.

51.  **Let a Headstart program use church facilities five days a week.**

I would strongly approve ............................. 1    [49]
I would approve ...................................... 2
I would disapprove .................................. 3
I would strongly disapprove ...................... 4

IF YOU WOULD DISAPPROVE, OR STRONGLY DISAPPROVE
51a.  Which *one* of the following is the *strongest* expression of disapproval you would be willing to make (if necessary) in this instance.

I would *not* openly express my disapproval in this instance ............................. 01 [50-51]
Discuss the matter with the minister .......... 02
Enlist the support of other members of the local church ............................. 03
Write a letter of protest to a principal officer of the local church ............... 04
Write a letter of protest to a denominational official ............................. 05
Bring the matter before the official board, or similar body ............................. 06
Attempt to have the minister dismissed .... 07
Stay away from church services ................ 08
Withhold donations and pledges .............. 09
Join another local church ........................ 10

52.  **Provided space in the church for meetings of welfare mothers seeking to challenge rulings of public welfare agencies.**

I would strongly approve ............................. 1    [52]
I would approve ...................................... 2
I would disapprove .................................. 3
I would strongly disapprove ...................... 4

IF YOU WOULD DISAPPROVE OR STRONGLY DISAPPROVE
52a.  Which *one* of the following is the *strongest* expression of disapproval you would be willing to make (if necessary) in this instance.

I would *not* openly express my disapproval in this instance ............................. 01 [53-54]
Discuss the matter with the minister .......... 02
Enlist the support of other members of the local church ............................. 03
Write a letter of protest to a principal officer of the local church ............... 04
Write a letter of protest to a denominational official ............................. 05
Bring the matter before the official board, or similar body ............................. 06
Attempt to have the minister dismissed ...... 07
Stay away from church services ................ 08
Withhold donations and pledges .............. 09
Join another local church ........................ 10

53.  **Participated with poor persons in a non-violent demonstration protesting treatment of the poor by welfare agencies.**

I would strongly approve ............................. 1    [55]
I would approve ...................................... 2
I would disapprove .................................. 3
I would strongly disapprove ...................... 4

IF YOU WOULD DISAPPROVE OR STRONGLY DISAPPROVE
53a.  Which *one* of the following is the *strongest* expression of disapproval you would be willing to make (if necessary) in this instance.

I would *not* openly express my disapproval in this instance ............................. 01 [56-57]
Discuss the matter with the minister .......... 02
Enlist the support of other members of the local church ............................. 03
Write a letter of protest to a principal officer of the local church ............... 04

Write a letter of protest to a denomina-
tional official ............................................. 05
Bring the matter before the official board,
or similar body .......................................... 06
Attempt to have the minister dismissed ...... 07
Stay away from church services ................... 08
Withhold donations and pledges ................. 09
Join another local church .......................... 10

**54.** Sent a representative to a group formed to monitor welfare agencies to be sure that no morally unfit person received public aid.

I would strongly approve .................... 1    [58]
I would approve ............................... 2
I would disapprove ........................... 3
I would strongly disapprove ............... 4

IF YOU WOULD DISAPPROVE OR STRONGLY DIS-
APPROVE
54a. Which *one* of the following is the *strongest* expression of disapproval you would be willing to make (if necessary) in this instance.

I would *not* openly express my disapproval
in this instance ......................................... 01 [59-60]
Discuss the matter with the minister ........... 02
Enlist the support of other members of the
local church ............................................... 03
Write a letter of protest to a principal
officer of the local church ....................... 04
Write a letter of protest to a denomina-
tional official ............................................. 05
Bring the matter before the official board,
or similar body .......................................... 06
Attempt to have the minister dismissed ....... 07
Stay away from church services ................... 08
Withhold donations and pledges ................. 09
Join another local church .......................... 10
[731 ................................. .03]

**55.** Contributed funds to a welfare rights organization.
I would strongly approve .................... 1    [10]
I would approve ............................... 2
I would disapprove ........................... 3
I would strongly disapprove ............... 4

IF YOU WOULD DISAPPROVE OR STRONGLY DIS-
APPROVE
55a. Which *one* of the following is the *strongest* expression of disapproval you would be willing to make (if necessary) in this instance.

I would *not* openly express my disapproval
in this instance ......................................... 01 [11-12]
Discuss the matter with the minister ........... 02
Enlist the support of other members of the
local church ............................................... 03
Write a letter of protest to a principal
officer of the local church ....................... 04
Write a letter of protest to a denomina-
tional official ............................................. 05
Bring the matter before the official board,
or similar body .......................................... 06
Attempt to have the minister dismissed ....... 07
Stay away from church services ................... 08
Withhold donations and pledges ................. 09
Join another local church .......................... 10

**56.** Provided space in the church for meetings of the local chapter of the National Association for the Advancement of Colored People.
I would strongly approve .................... 1    [13]
I would approve ............................... 2
I would disapprove ........................... 3
I would strongly disapprove ............... 4

IF YOU WOULD DISAPPROVE OR STRONGLY DIS-
APPROVE
56a. Which *one* of the following is the *strongest* expression of disapproval you would be willing to make (if necessary) in this instance.

I would *not* openly express my disapproval
in this instance ......................................... 01 [14-15]
Discuss the matter with the minister ........... 02
Enlist the support of other members of the
local church ............................................... 03
Write a letter of protest to a principal
officer of the local church ....................... 04
Write a letter of protest to a denomina-
tional official ............................................. 05
Bring the matter before the official board,
or similar body .......................................... 06
Attempt to have the minister dismissed ...... 07
Stay away from church services ................... 08
Withhold donations and pledges ................. 09
Join another local church .......................... 10

**57.** Contributed money to a minority group in response to the demand that churches pay reparations for their part in discrimination against that group.
I would strongly approve .................... 1    [16]
I would approve ............................... 2
I would disapprove ........................... 3
I would strongly disapprove ............... 4

IF YOU WOULD DISAPPROVE OR STRONGLY DIS-
APPROVE
57a. Which *one* of the following is the *strongest* expression of disapproval you would be willing to make (if necessary) in this instance.

I would *not* openly express my disapproval
in this instance ......................................... 01 [17-18]
Discuss the matter with the minister ........... 02
Enlist the support of other members of
the local church ......................................... 03
Write a letter of protest to a principal
officer of the local church ....................... 04
Write a letter of protest to a denomina-
tional official ............................................. 05
Bring the matter before the official board,
or similar body .......................................... 06
Attempt to have the minister dismissed ....... 07
Stay away from church services ................... 08
Withhold donations and pledges ................. 09
Join another local church .......................... 10

**58.** Secured a black as senior minister.
I would strongly approve .................... 1    [19]
I would approve ............................... 2
I would disapprove ........................... 3
I would strongly disapprove ............... 4

IF YOU WOULD DISAPPROVE OR STRONGLY DIS-
APPROVE
58a. Which *one* of the following is the *strongest* expression of disapproval you would be willing to make (if necessary) in this instance.

I would *not* openly express my disapproval
in this instance ......................................... 01 [20-21]
Discuss the matter with the minister ........... 02
Enlist the support of other members in
the local church ......................................... 03
Write a letter of protest to a principal
officer of the local church ....................... 04
Write a letter of protest to a denomina-
tional official ............................................. 05

Bring the matter before the official board,
or similar body .............................. 06
Attempt to have the minister dismissed ........ 07
Stay away from church services .................. 08
Withhold donations and pledges .............. 09
Join another local church .......................... 10

**59. Contributed money to a group formed to keep blacks out of the church's neighborhood.**
I would strongly approve ........................... 1  [22]
I would approve ...................................... 2
I would disapprove ................................. 3
I would strongly disapprove ........................ 4

IF YOU WOULD DISAPPROVE OR STRONGLY DIS-
APPROVE
59a. Which *one* of the following is the *strongest* expression of disapproval you would be willing to make (if necessary) in this instance.
I would *not* openly express my disapproval
in this instance .......................... 01  [23-24]
Discuss the matter with the minister ........... 02
Enlist the support of other members of
the local church ..................................... 03
Write a letter of protest to a principal
officer of the local church ....................... 04
Write a letter of protest to a denomina-
tional official ..................................... 05
Bring the matter before the official board,
or similar body ................................. 06
Attempt to have the minister dismissed ........ 07
Stay away from church services .................. 08
Withhold donations and pledges .............. 09
Join another local church .......................... 10

**60. Made a public appeal for unconditional amnesty for all those who evaded the draft during the Vietnam war.**
I would strongly approve ........................... 1  [25]
I would approve ...................................... 2
I would disapprove ................................. 3
I would strongly disapprove ........................ 4

IF YOU WOULD DISAPPROVE OR STRONGLY DIS-
APPROVE
60a. Which *one* of the following is the *strongest* expression of disapproval you would be willing to make (if necessary) in this instance.
I would *not* openly express my disapproval
in this instance .......................... 01  [26-27]
Discuss the matter with the minister ........... 02
Enlist the support of other members of
the local church ..................................... 03
Write a letter of protest to a principal
officer of the local church ....................... 04
Write a letter of protest to a denomina-
tional official ..................................... 05
Bring the matter before the official board,
or similar body ................................. 06
Attempt to have the minister dismissed ...... 07
Stay away from church services .................. 08
Withhold donations and pledges .............. 09
Join another local church .......................... 10

**61. Took a special offering for the reconstruction of North Vietnam.**
I would strongly approve ........................... 1  [28]
I would approve ...................................... 2
I would disapprove ................................. 3
I would strongly disapprove ........................ 4

IF YOU WOULD DISAPPROVE OR STRONGLY DIS-
APPROVE
61a. Which *one* of the following is the *strongest* expression of disapproval you would be willing to make (if necessary) in this instance.
I would *not* openly express my disapproval
in this instance .......................... 01  [29-30]
Discuss the matter with the minister ........... 02
Enlist the support of other members of
the local church ..................................... 03
Write a letter of protest to a principal
officer of the local church ....................... 04
Write a letter of protest to a denomina-
tional official ..................................... 05
Bring the matter before the official board,
or similar body ................................. 06
Attempt to have the minister dismissed ........ 07
Stay away from church services .................. 08
Withhold donations and pledges .............. 09
Join another local church .......................... 10

**62. Let a birth control clinic use church facilities.**
I would strongly approve ........................... 1  [31]
I would approve ...................................... 2
I would disapprove ................................. 3
I would strongly disapprove ........................ 4

IF YOU WOULD DISAPPROVE OR STRONGLY DIS-
APPROVE
62a. Which *one* of the following is the *strongest* expression of disapproval you would be willing to make (if necessary) in this instance.
I would *not* openly express my disapproval
in this instance .......................... 01  [32-33]
Discuss the matter with the minister ........... 02
Enlist the support of other members
of the local church ............................... 03
Write a letter of protest to a principal
officer of the local church ....................... 04
Write a letter of protest to a denomina-
tional official ..................................... 05
Bring the matter before the official board,
or similar body ................................. 06
Attempt to have the minister dismissed ........ 07
Stay away from church services .................. 08
Withhold donations and pledges .............. 09
Join another local church .......................... 10

**63. Provided information to women seeking legal abortions.**
I would strongly approve ........................... 1  [34]
I would approve ...................................... 2
I would disapprove ................................. 3
I would strongly disapprove ........................ 4

IF YOU WOULD DISAPPROVE OR STRONGLY DIS-
APPROVE
63a. Which *one* of the following is the *strongest* expression of disapproval you would be willing to make (if necessary) in this instance.
I would *not* openly express my disapproval
in this instance .......................... 01  [35-36]
Discuss the matter with the minister ........... 02
Enlist the support of other members
of the local church ............................... 03
Write a letter of protest to a principal
officer of the local church ....................... 04
Write a letter of protest to a denomina-
tional official ..................................... 05

Bring the matter before the official board,
or similar body ............................................. 06
Attempt to have the minister dismissed ...... 07
Stay away from church services ................... 08
Withhold donations and pledges ................. 09
Join another local church ............................ 10

**64. Publicly endorsed busing of school children for the purpose of achieving a racial balance in Indianapolis schools.**
I would strongly approve ............................. 1     [37]
I would approve .......................................... 2
I would disapprove ...................................... 3
I would strongly disapprove ........................ 4

IF YOU WOULD DISAPPROVE OR STRONGLY DIS-
APPROVE
64a.  Which *one* of the following is the *strongest* expression of disapproval you would be willing to make (if necessary) in this instance.
I would *not* openly express my disapproval
in this instance ........................................... 01  [38-39]
Discuss the matter with the minister ........... 02
Enlist the support of other members
of the local church ..................................... 03
Write a letter of protest to a principal
officer of the local church ......................... 04
Write a letter of protest to a denomina-
tional official ............................................. 05
Bring the matter before the official board,
or similar body ........................................... 06
Attempt to have the minister dismissed ........ 07
Stay away from church services ................... 08
Withhold donations and pledges ................. 09
Join another local church ............................ 10

**65. Publicly opposed busing of school children for the purpose of achieving a racial balance in Indianapolis schools.**
I would strongly approve ............................. 1     [40]
I would approve .......................................... 2
I would disapprove ...................................... 3
I would strongly disapprove ........................ 4

IF YOU WOULD DISAPPROVE OR STRONGLY DIS-
APPROVE
65a.  Which *one* of the following is the *strongest* expression of disapproval you would be willing to make (if necessary) in this instance.
I would *not* openly express my disapproval
in this instance ........................................... 01  [41-42]
Discuss the matter with the minister ........... 02
Enlist the support of other members
of the local church ..................................... 03
Write a letter of protest to a principal
officer of the local church ......................... 04
Write a letter of protest to a denomina-
tional official ............................................. 05
Bring the matter before the official board,
or similar body ........................................... 06
Attempt to have the minister dismissed ........ 07
Stay away from church services ................... 08
Withhold donations and pledges ................. 09
Join another local church ............................ 10

**66. Joined with other organizations in the community to push for legal action against a local factory which persisted in polluting the environment.**
I would strongly approve ............................. 1     [43]
I would approve .......................................... 2
I would disapprove ...................................... 3
I would strongly disapprove ........................ 4

IF YOU WOULD DISAPPROVE OR STRONGLY DIS-
APPROVE
66a.  Which *one* of the following is the *strongest* expression of disapproval you would be willing to make (if necessary) in this instance.
I would *not* openly express my disapproval
in this instance ........................................... 01  [44-45]
Discuss the matter with the minister ........... 02
Enlist the support of other members
of the local church ..................................... 03
Write a letter of protest to a principal
officer of the local church ......................... 04
Write a letter of protest to a denomina-
tional official ............................................. 05
Bring the matter before the official board,
or similar body ........................................... 06
Attempt to have the minister dismissed ........ 07
Stay away from church services ................... 08
Withhold donations and pledges ............... 09
Join another local church ............................ 10

**67. Publicly endorsed equal rights for women.**
I would strongly approve ............................. 1     [46]
I would approve .......................................... 2
I would disapprove ...................................... 3
I would strongly disapprove ........................ 4

IF YOU WOULD DISAPPROVE OR STRONGLY DIS-
APPROVE
67a.  Which *one* of the following is the *strongest* expression of disapproval you would be willing to make (if necessary) in this instance.
I would *not* openly express my disapproval
in this instance ........................................... 01  [47-48]
Discuss the matter with the minister ........... 02
Enlist the support of other members
of the local church ..................................... 03
Write a letter of protest to a principal
officer of the local church ......................... 04
Write a letter of protest to a denomina-
tional official ............................................. 05
Bring the matter before the official board,
or similar body ........................................... 06
Attempt to have the minister dismissed ...... 07
Stay away from church services ................... 08
Withhold donations and pledges ................. 09
Join another local church ............................ 10

**68. Secured a woman as senior minister.**
I would strongly approve ............................. 1     [49]
I would approve .......................................... 2
I would disapprove ...................................... 3
I would strongly disapprove ........................ 4

IF YOU WOULD DISAPPROVE OR STRONGLY DIS-
APPROVE
68a.  Which *one* of the following is the *strongest* expression of disapproval you would be willing to make (if necessary) in this instance.
I would *not* openly express my disapproval
in this instance ........................................... 01  [50-51]
Discuss the matter with the minister ........... 02
Enlist the support of other members
of the local church ..................................... 03
Write a letter of protest to a principal
officer of the local church ......................... 04
Write a letter of protest to a denomina-
tional official ............................................. 05
Bring the matter before the official board,
or similar body ........................................... 06
Attempt to have the minister dismissed ....... 07
Stay away from church services ................... 08
Withhold donations and pledges ................. 09
Join another local church ............................ 10

**69. Publicly identified with a strike for fairer treatment of employees of a local factory or business.**

I would strongly approve ............................ 1    [52]
I would approve ........................................ 2
I would disapprove .................................. 3
I would strongly disapprove ...................... 4

IF YOU WOULD DISAPPROVE OR STRONGLY DISAPPROVE

69a. Which *one* of the following is the *strongest* expression of disapproval you would be willing to make (if necessary) in this instance.

I would *not* openly express my disapproval
in this instance ............................................ 01    [53-54]
Discuss the matter with the minister ............ 02
Enlist the support of other members
of the local church .................................... 03
Write a letter of protest to a principal
officer of the local church ........................ 04
Write a letter of protest to a denomina-
tional official ............................................ 05
Bring the matter before the official board,
or similar body ........................................ 06
Attempt to have the minister dismissed ........ 07
Stay away from church services .................... 08
Withhold donations and pledges ................ 09
Join another local church ............................ 10

**70. Held a marriage ceremony for an interracial couple.**

I would strongly approve ............................ 1    [55]
I would approve ........................................ 2
I would disapprove .................................. 3
I would strongly disapprove ...................... 4

IF YOU WOULD DISAPPROVE OR STRONGLY DISAPPROVE

70a. Which *one* of the following is the *strongest* expression of disapproval you would be willing to make (if necessary) in this instance.

I would *not* openly express my disapproval
in this instance ............................................ 01    [56-57]
Discuss the matter with the minister ............ 02
Enlist the support of other members
of the local church .................................... 03
Write a letter of protest to a principal
officer of the local church ........................ 04
Write a letter of protest to a denomina-
tional official ............................................ 05
Bring the matter before the official board,
or similar body ........................................ 06
Attempt to have the minister dismissed ........ 07
Stay away from church services .................... 08
Withhold donations and pledges ................ 09
Join another local church ............................ 10

**VI.** Now we are interested in your ideas about the role of your minister. (If your church has more than one minister, you should answer with reference to the senior minister.)

[731............................04]

71. The following activities are possible ways in which your minister could spend his time. Please look over the list of activities, then answer the questions below.

01   Charity work
02   Teaching
03   Planning worship services

04   Evangelism
05   Administrative work
06   Creating an atmosphere of warmth and friendliness within the local church
07   Preparing sermons and preaching
08   Offering comfort to those in sorrow and in need
09   Speaking out against social issues, such as poverty
10   Taking a stand on moral issues such as abortion
11   Involvement in political issues
12   Sponsoring social activities for members of the local church such as picnics
13   Providing spiritual guidance for members of the local church

Enter the number of the ministerial
activity you think *your minister*
considers *most important* ........................——— [10-11]

Enter here the number of the ministerial
activity you *personally* consider *most*
*important* ................................................ ——— [12-13]

72. Do you believe that your minister holds the same views on social policies as most of your congregation?

Yes .................................................... 1    [14]
No .................................................... 2

IF NO

72a. Would you say he is more "conservative" or more "liberal"?

More conservative ................................ 1    [15]
More liberal ........................................ 2

72b. Do you think your minister is aware that he differs?

Yes .................................................... 1    [16]
No .................................................... 2

73. Do you feel that decisions for directing the local church's activities in the surrounding community are decided more by the denomination, the minister, the official board, or members at large?

Denomination .................................... 1    [17]
Minister .............................................. 2
Official board .................................... 3
Members at large ................................ 4

Here are some things people have said about ministers. Do you agree or disagree?

74. Ministers have a responsibility to speak out as the moral conscience of the nation.

Strongly agree .................................... 1    [18]
Agree .................................................. 2
Disagree .............................................. 3
Strongly disagree ................................ 4

75. Ministers should behave according to the expectations of their congregations.

Strongly agree .................................... 1    [19]
Agree .................................................. 2
Disagree .............................................. 3
Strongly disagree ................................ 4

76. I want my minister to preach the gospel no matter whose toes he steps on.

Strongly agree .................................... 1    [20]
Agree .................................................. 2
Disagree .............................................. 3
Strongly disagree ................................ 4

77. Ministers should stick to religion and not concern themselves with social, economic, and political questions.

Strongly agree ............................................... 1   [21]
Agree ................................................................ 2
Disagree .......................................................... 3
Strongly disagree ........................................... 4

78. My minister is someone I feel I could turn to with my problems.

Strongly agree ............................................... 1   [22]
Agree ................................................................ 2
Disagree .......................................................... 3
Strongly disagree ........................................... 4

79. I would support my minister if he were to participate in a picket line or demonstration on behalf of underprivileged people.

Strongly agree ............................................... 1   [23]
Agree ................................................................ 2
Disagree .......................................................... 3
Strongly disagree ........................................... 4

80. A minister should not publicly express views which are contrary to the views of the majority of the congregation.

Strongly agree ............................................... 1   [24]
Agree ................................................................ 2
Disagree .......................................................... 3
Strongly disagree ........................................... 4

81. Ministers today are more responsive to their members' needs than ever before.

Strongly agree ............................................... 1   [25]
Agree ................................................................ 2
Disagree .......................................................... 3
Strongly disagree ........................................... 4

82. I am happy for my minister to participate actively in social controversies.

Strongly agree ............................................... 1   [26]
Agree ................................................................ 2
Disagree .......................................................... 3
Strongly disagree ........................................... 4

83. Even if a minister does a poor job, he should be supported out of respect for the position he holds.

Strongly agree ............................................... 1   [27]
Agree ................................................................ 2
Disagree .......................................................... 3
Strongly disagree ........................................... 4

84. I want my minister to feel free to give a sermon on any social or political issue he strongly supports.

Strongly agree ............................................... 1   [28]
Agree ................................................................ 2
Disagree .......................................................... 3
Strongly disagree ........................................... 4

85. Considering your minister's sermons in general, do you

Agree with them ........................................... 1   [29]
Mostly agree with them ............................... 2
Mostly disagree with them .......................... 3
Disagree with them ....................................... 4

VII. Let's turn now to questions about your denomination (the national body with which your local church is affiliated).

86. Think for a moment about your denomination. What single thing do you like best about your denomination?

Its concern with saving souls ...................... 01 [30-31]
The democratic form of its government .... 02
The hierarchic form of its government ....... 03
Its involvement in social action .................. 04
Its ecumenism, trying to merge with
other denominations ...................................... 05
Its liberal theology ......................................... 06
Its conservative theology ............................. 07
Its theological diversity ................................. 08
The informality of its type of worship ....... 09
The formality of its type of worship ......... 10
An educated ministry ..................................... 11
An emphasis on world missions ................. 12

87. Do you read denominational literature frequently, occasionally, rarely or never?

Frequently ........................................................ 1   [32]
Occasionally ..................................................... 2
Rarely ............................................................... 3
Never ................................................................ 4

88. Are you generally satisfied with the job your denominational officials are doing?

Yes .................................................................... 1   [33]
No ...................................................................... 2

89. Are you generally satisfied with the procedures your denomination uses to arrive at its positions on social issues?

Yes .................................................................... 1   [34]
No ...................................................................... 2

IF NO

89a. What is the *main* thing you would like to see changed?
[35-36]

If you happen to know the position of your denomination or its principal agencies regarding the following public issues, please indicate the response which best describes that position.

90. Project Equality; an interdenominational alliance of churches and church institutions pledged to do business only with firms practicing fair employment with regard to Negroes.

Don't know ...................................................... 1   [37]
Denomination approves of Project
Equality ........................................................... 2
Denomination has no position ..................... 3
Denomination disapproves of Project
Equality ........................................................... 4

91. Busing.

Don't know ...................................................... 1   [38]
Denomination favors the use of busing
as a means of desegregation ...................... 2
Denomination has no official position ........ 3
Denomination is opposed to the use
of busing as a means of desegregation ......... 4

92. Legalized abortion.

Don't know ...................................................... 1   [39]
Denomination favors Supreme Court
decision on abortion ..................................... 2
Denomination has no official position ......... 3
Denomination opposes Supreme Court
decision on abortion ..................................... 4

93. Women's rights.
    Don't know ................................................ 1    [40]
    Denomination favors the idea of equal
    rights for women, but is opposed to
    hard-line women's liberation groups .............. 2
    Denomination favors equal rights for
    women and supports women's libera-
    ation groups (*not* financially) ........................ 3
    Denomination has no official position ......... 4
    Denomination is opposed to equal
    rights for women ......................................... 5

94. Reconstruction of Vietnamese society.
    Don't know ................................................ 1    [41]
    Denomination supports the idea that the
    U.S. should help in the rebuilding of
    Vietnamese society (both in North and
    South Vietnam) ........................................... 2
    Denomination supports the idea that the
    U.S. should help in the rebuilding of
    Vietnamese society (both the North
    and South) and provides funds to do so ...... 3
    Denomination believes that the U.S.
    should *not* help in the rebuilding of
    Vietnamese society ...................................... 4
    Denomination has no official position ............ 5

95. Social responsibility of corporations.
    Don't know ................................................ 1    [42]
    Denomination favors the idea that big
    businesses should be concerned with
    social issues relating to business such as
    pollution, equal employment oppor-
    tunities, etc. ................................................ 2
    Denomination favors the philosophy
    of social responsibility of big business
    and advocates the withdrawal of in-
    vestments from businesses which are
    not concerned with the issues of
    pollution, equal opportunity employment,
    etc. ............................................................. 3
    Denomination believes that the church
    should *not* enter into worldly affairs
    such as the social responsibility of
    big businesses .............................................. 4
    Denomination has no official position ............ 5

96. Several denominations have been considering coming together to form a new denomination called the Church of Christ
Uniting (the group of denominations has been called the Con-
sultation on Church Union).
Is your denomination one of these?
    Yes ............................................................. 1    [43]
    No .............................................................. 2
    I don't know ............................................... 3
IF YES
96a. Are you pleased that your denomination is included?
    Yes ............................................................. 1    [44]
    No .............................................................. 2
IF NO or DON'T KNOW
96b. Would you like your denomination to be a part of these
negotiations?
    Yes ............................................................. 1    [45]
    No .............................................................. 2

VIII.  Here are a number of statements which people
have made about various aspects of the church. Please
indicate the extent of your agreement or disagreement.

97. The church should direct some of its activities toward
changing the structure of American society.
    Strongly agree ............................................. 1    [46]
    Agree .......................................................... 2
    Disagree ...................................................... 3
    Strongly disagree ......................................... 4

98. The local church (rather than the denomination) is always the best judge of who should be admitted to its membership.
    Strongly agree ............................................. 1    [47]
    Agree .......................................................... 2
    Disagree ...................................................... 3
    Strongly disagree ......................................... 4

99. It is the church's primary job to provide comfort to its
members in time of need.
    Strongly agree ............................................. 1    [48]
    Agree .......................................................... 2
    Disagree ...................................................... 3
    Strongly disagree ......................................... 4

100. Membership in my local church gives me a chance to
associate with people like myself.
    Strongly agree ............................................. 1    [49]
    Agree .......................................................... 2
    Disagree ...................................................... 3
    Strongly disagree ......................................... 4

101. My first loyalty is to my local church, not to the
denomination.
    Strongly agree ............................................. 1    [50]
    Agree .......................................................... 2
    Disagree ...................................................... 3
    Strongly disagree ......................................... 4

102. It is not right for a local church to disregard the counsel
of denominational leaders.
    Strongly agree ............................................. 1    [51]
    Agree .......................................................... 2
    Disagree ...................................................... 3
    Strongly disagree ......................................... 4

103. The denomination's position *should* carry most weight in
determining my local church's involvement in social issues.
    Strongly agree ............................................. 1    [52]
    Agree .......................................................... 2
    Disagree ...................................................... 3
    Strongly disagree ......................................... 4

104. My denomination is an important influence on my
attitudes toward social issues.
    Strongly agree ............................................. 1    [53]
    Agree .......................................................... 2
    Disagree ...................................................... 3
    Strongly disagree ......................................... 4

105. I want my local church to be closely tied with the
denomination.
    Strongly agree ............................................. 1    [54]
    Agree .......................................................... 2
    Disagree ...................................................... 3
    Strongly disagree ......................................... 4

106. On social action issues, each local church should make its own decisions.

Strongly agree ............................................. 1    [55]
Agree .............................................................. 2
Disagree ......................................................... 3
Strongly disagree .......................................... 4

107. I wish my local church were not so much under the influence of the denomination.

Strongly agree ............................................. 1    [56]
Agree .............................................................. 2
Disagree ......................................................... 3
Strongly disagree .......................................... 4

108. I would be distressed if my local church were to withdraw from the denomination.

Strongly agree ............................................. 1    [57]
Agree .............................................................. 2
Disagree ......................................................... 3
Strongly disagree .......................................... 4

109. My local church is an important influence on my attitude toward social issues.

Strongly agree ............................................. 1    [58]
Agree .............................................................. 2
Disagree ......................................................... 3
Strongly disagree .......................................... 4

110. Even when I disagree, I feel a moral obligation to support the social policies of my denomination.

Strongly agree ............................................. 1    [59]
Agree .............................................................. 2
Disagree ......................................................... 3
Strongly disagree .......................................... 4

111. Denominational leaders should respect the right of local churches to make their own decisions no matter what the issue.

Strongly agree ............................................. 1    [60]
Agree .............................................................. 2
Disagree ......................................................... 3
Strongly disagree .......................................... 4

112. My denomination should censure local churches which refuse to accept black members.

Strongly agree ............................................. 1    [61]
Agree .............................................................. 2
Disagree ......................................................... 3
Strongly disagree .......................................... 4

113. If policies of my local church and denomination were in conflict on some issue, I would feel obligated to follow the denomination's policies.

Strongly agree ............................................. 1    [62]
Agree .............................................................. 2
Disagree ......................................................... 3
Strongly disagree .......................................... 4

114. For the most part, the churches have been woefully inadequate in facing up to the civil rights issue.

Strongly agree ............................................. 1    [63]
Agree .............................................................. 2
Disagree ......................................................... 3
Strongly disagree .......................................... 4

115. The sole responsibility to my denomination is to provide spiritual guidance for its members.

Strongly agree ............................................. 1    [64]
Agree .............................................................. 2
Disagree ......................................................... 3
Strongly disagree .......................................... 4

[731..............................05]

116. Churches should refuse to do business with firms unwilling to hire blacks on the same basis as whites.

Strongly agree ............................................. 1    [10]
Agree .............................................................. 2
Disagree ......................................................... 3
Strongly disagree .......................................... 4

117. I am always happy to tell people the denomination I belong to.

Strongly agree ............................................. 1    [11]
Agree .............................................................. 2
Disagree ......................................................... 3
Strongly disagree .......................................... 4

118. The central interests of my life are not closely related to the church.

Strongly agree ............................................. 1    [12]
Agree .............................................................. 2
Disagree ......................................................... 3
Strongly disagree .......................................... 4

119. The church should only engage in activities which are approved of by the majority of its members.

Strongly agree ............................................. 1    [13]
Agree .............................................................. 2
Disagree ......................................................... 3
Strongly disagree .......................................... 4

120. A local church should limit its membership to those people who would get along well with other members.

Strongly agree ............................................. 1    [14]
Agree .............................................................. 2
Disagree ......................................................... 3
Strongly disagree .......................................... 4

121. Denominations should urge their local churches to admit Negroes to membership.

Strongly agree ............................................. 1    [15]
Agree .............................................................. 2
Disagree ......................................................... 3
Strongly disagree .......................................... 4

122. Denominations should use their corporate power to change the structure of our society.

Strongly agree ............................................. 1    [16]
Agree .............................................................. 2
Disagree ......................................................... 3
Strongly disagree .......................................... 4

123. At all levels of the church, utmost care should be taken not to introduce controversy into the church.

Strongly agree ............................................. 1    [17]
Agree .............................................................. 2
Disagree ......................................................... 3
Strongly disagree .......................................... 4

124. I am proud that my denomination speaks out against social injustice, such as racial discrimination and poverty.

Strongly agree ............................................. 1    [18]
Agree .............................................................. 2
Disagree ......................................................... 3
Strongly disagree .......................................... 4

125. A local church should never engage in any activities which would cause important people in the community to respect its members less.

Strongly agree ............................................. 1    [19]
Agree .............................................................. 2
Disagree ......................................................... 3
Strongly disagree .......................................... 4

126. My local church should concern itself with the problems and needs of its members rather than with social and political problems.
Strongly agree ............................................. 1    [20]
Agree ............................................................ 2
Disagree ....................................................... 3
Strongly disagree ........................................ 4

127. My local church is a source of comfort to me in a world filled with troubles.
Strongly agree ............................................. 1    [21]
Agree ............................................................ 2
Disagree ....................................................... 3
Strongly disagree ........................................ 4

128. A *local church* should not engage in any activities which might cause it to lose members.
Strongly agree ............................................. 1    [22]
Agree ............................................................ 2
Disagree ....................................................... 3
Strongly disagree ........................................ 4

129. To be perfectly honest, I don't care what my local church says or does about social issues.
Strongly agree ............................................. 1    [23]
Agree ............................................................ 2
Disagree ....................................................... 3
Strongly disagree ........................................ 4

130. My denomination should not take a stand on controversial issues which might divide its members.
Strongly agree ............................................. 1    [24]
Agree ............................................................ 2
Disagree ....................................................... 3
Strongly disagree ........................................ 4

131. The best way my denomination can work to solve social problems is through its missionary and charitable works.
Strongly agree ............................................. 1    [25]
Agree ............................................................ 2
Disagree ....................................................... 3
Strongly disagree ........................................ 4

132. It is not the responsibility of my denomination to try to solve social problems like poverty and discrimination.
Strongly agree ............................................. 1    [26]
Agree ............................................................ 2
Disagree ....................................................... 3
Strongly disagree ........................................ 4

133. My denomination should take a stand on moral issues like abortion.
Strongly agree ............................................. 1    [27]
Agree ............................................................ 2
Disagree ....................................................... 3
Strongly disagree ........................................ 4

134. My denomination should stick to religion and not concern itself with social and political problems.
Strongly agree ............................................. 1    [28]
Agree ............................................................ 2
Disagree ....................................................... 3
Strongly disagree ........................................ 4

135. My denomination should use its resources to fight social injustice.
Strongly agree ............................................. 1    [29]
Agree ............................................................ 2
Disagree ....................................................... 3
Strongly disagree ........................................ 4

136. It is the responsibility of my denomination to speak out against social injustices which exist in our country.
Strongly agree ............................................. 1    [30]
Agree ............................................................ 2
Disagree ....................................................... 3
Strongly disagree ........................................ 4

IX. This section deals with current affairs and public issues.

137. The following is a list of reasons some people give to explain why there are poor people in this country. Please indicate how important *you* think each reason is in explaining poverty in America.
a. Lack of thrift and proper money management by poor people.
Very important ............................................. 1    [31]
Somewhat important .................................... 2
Not important .............................................. 3
b. Lack of effort by the poor themselves.
Very important ............................................. 1    [32]
Somewhat important .................................... 2
Not important .............................................. 3
c. Lack of ability and talent among poor people.
Very important ............................................. 1    [33]
Somewhat important .................................... 2
Not important .............................................. 3
d. Loose morals and drunkenness.
Very important ............................................. 1    [34]
Somewhat important .................................... 2
Not important .............................................. 3
e. Sickness and physical handicaps.
Very important ............................................. 1    [35]
Somewhat important .................................... 2
Not important .............................................. 3
f. Low wages in some businesses and industries.
Very important ............................................. 1    [36]
Somewhat important .................................... 2
Not important .............................................. 3
g. Failure of society to provide good schools for many Americans.
Very important ............................................. 1    [37]
Somewhat important .................................... 2
Not important .............................................. 3
h. Prejudice and discrimination against blacks.
Very important ............................................. 1    [38]
Somewhat important .................................... 2
Not important .............................................. 3
i. Failure of private industry to provide enough jobs.
Very important ............................................. 1    [39]
Somewhat important .................................... 2
Not important .............................................. 3
j. Being taken advantage of by rich people.
Very important ............................................. 1    [40]
Somewhat important .................................... 2
Not important .............................................. 3
k. Just bad luck.
Very important ............................................. 1    [41]
Somewhat important .................................... 2
Not important .............................................. 3

Here is a series of statements on current affairs and public issues with which some people agree and some disagree. Please indicate how you feel about each of these statements. (Circle the number after the response which comes closest to how you feel.)

138. Environmental pollution is not as important as it's been made out to be.
Strongly agree ............................................. 1    [42]
Agree ............................................. 2
Disagree ............................................. 3
Strongly disagree ............................................. 4

139. Abortion must be a personal and medical decision only.
Strongly agree ............................................. 1    [43]
Agree ............................................. 2
Disagree ............................................. 3
Strongly disagree ............................................. 4

140. Labor unions do this country more harm than good.
Strongly agree ............................................. 1    [44]
Agree ............................................. 2
Disagree ............................................. 3
Strongly disagree ............................................. 4

141. Every American ought to take a bold stand in protecting freedom of speech even for Communists.
Strongly agree ............................................. 1    [45]
Agree ............................................. 2
Disagree ............................................. 3
Strongly disagree ............................................. 4

142. Church supported elementary schools should receive government financial aid.
Strongly agree ............................................. 1    [46]
Agree ............................................. 2
Disagree ............................................. 3
Strongly disagree ............................................. 4

143. Teachers should be allowed to go on strike.
Strongly agree ............................................. 1    [47]
Agree ............................................. 2
Disagree ............................................. 3
Strongly disagree ............................................. 4

144. Homosexuals are criminal and should be treated as such.
Strongly agree ............................................. 1    [48]
Agree ............................................. 2
Disagree ............................................. 3
Strongly disagree ............................................. 4

145. I can understand why black people are sometimes driven to violence.
Strongly agree ............................................. 1    [49]
Agree ............................................. 2
Disagree ............................................. 3
Strongly disagree ............................................. 4

146. I am glad that Red China was finally admitted to the United Nations.
Strongly agree ............................................. 1    [50]
Agree ............................................. 2
Disagree ............................................. 3
Strongly disagree ............................................. 4

147. There are too many people receiving welfare money who could work if they were willing.
Strongly agree ............................................. 1    [51]
Agree ............................................. 2
Disagree ............................................. 3
Strongly disagree ............................................. 4

148. The church should pay taxes even on buildings used primarily for religious purposes.
Strongly agree ............................................. 1    [52]
Agree ............................................. 2
Disagree ............................................. 3
Strongly disagree ............................................. 4

149. The U.S. Government should use the military if necessary to protect investments in underdeveloped countries.
Strongly agree ............................................. 1    [53]
Agree ............................................. 2
Disagree ............................................. 3
Strongly disagree ............................................. 4

150. In American society, any individual with ability and ambition can earn a good income.
Strongly agree ............................................. 1    [54]
Agree ............................................. 2
Disagree ............................................. 3
Strongly disagree ............................................. 4

151. Women, if they work at all, should take feminine positions such as nursing, secretarial work, or child care.
Strongly agree ............................................. 1    [55]
Agree ............................................. 2
Disagree ............................................. 3
Strongly disagree ............................................. 4

152. We are spending too *little* money on welfare programs in this country.
Strongly agree ............................................. 1    [56]
Agree ............................................. 2
Disagree ............................................. 3
Strongly disagree ............................................. 4

153. Drug users should be treated as sick people, rather than as criminals.
Strongly agree ............................................. 1    [57]
Agree ............................................. 2
Disagree ............................................. 3
Strongly disagree ............................................. 4

154. It was a mistake to stop the bombing in Cambodia.
Strongly agree ............................................. 1    [58]
Agree ............................................. 2
Disagree ............................................. 3
Strongly disagree ............................................. 4

155. No crime is serious enough to justify the death penalty.
Strongly agree ............................................. 1    [59]
Agree ............................................. 2
Disagree ............................................. 3
Strongly disagree ............................................. 4

156. The United States should withdraw from the United Nations.
Strongly agree ............................................. 1    [60]
Agree ............................................. 2
Disagree ............................................. 3
Strongly disagree ............................................. 4

157. Many people getting welfare misrepresent their financial needs.
Strongly agree ............................................. 1    [61]
Agree ............................................. 2
Disagree ............................................. 3
Strongly disagree ............................................. 4

158. Birth control methods should be readily available to *all* women.
      Strongly agree ............................................. 1    [62]
      Agree ........................................................ 2
      Disagree .................................................... 3
      Strongly disagree ...................................... 4

159. American churches should provide money for the economic advancement of black Americans.
      Strongly agree ............................................. 1    [63]
      Agree ........................................................ 2
      Disagree .................................................... 3
      Strongly disagree ...................................... 4

160. Most people on welfare who can work try to find jobs so that they can support themselves.
      Strongly agree ............................................. 1    [64]
      Agree ........................................................ 2
      Disagree .................................................... 3
      Strongly disagree ...................................... 4

161. The government should control private industry for the common good.
      Strongly agree ............................................. 1    [65]
      Agree ........................................................ 2
      Disagree .................................................... 3
      Strongly disagree ...................................... 4

162. Young men who left the United States to avoid the draft should be allowed to return to this country without any form of punishment.
      Strongly agree ............................................. 1    [66]
      Agree ........................................................ 2
      Disagree .................................................... 3
      Strongly disagree ...................................... 4

163. A guaranteed income would just give money to people who are too lazy to go out and work.
      Strongly agree ............................................. 1    [67]
      Agree ........................................................ 2
      Disagree .................................................... 3
      Strongly disagree ...................................... 4

164. One of the main troubles with welfare is that it doesn't give people enough money to get along on.
      Strongly agree ............................................. 1    [68]
      Agree ........................................................ 2
      Disagree .................................................... 3
      Strongly disagree ...................................... 4

165. It is the duty of a citizen to support his country, right or wrong.
      Strongly agree ............................................. 1    [69]
      Agree ........................................................ 2
      Disagree .................................................... 3
      Strongly disagree ...................................... 4

166. No decent man can respect a woman who has had sex relations before marriage.
      Strongly agree ............................................. 1    [70]
      Agree ........................................................ 2
      Disagree .................................................... 3
      Strongly disagree ...................................... 4

167. The law should allow doctors to perform an abortion for any woman who wants one.
      Strongly agree ............................................. 1    [71]
      Agree ........................................................ 2
      Disagree .................................................... 3
      Strongly disagree ...................................... 4

168. What young people need most of all is strict discipline by their parents.
      Strongly agree ............................................. 1    [72]
      Agree ........................................................ 2
      Disagree .................................................... 3
      Strongly disagree ...................................... 4

                                          [731................06]
169. A woman should not earn money in business or industry if she has a husband supporting her.
      Strongly agree ............................................. 1    [10]
      Agree ........................................................ 2
      Disagree .................................................... 3
      Strongly disagree ...................................... 4

170. A woman finds it difficult to be happy in life unless she marries and raises a family.
      Strongly agree ............................................. 1    [11]
      Agree ........................................................ 2
      Disagree .................................................... 3
      Strongly disagree ...................................... 4

171. I approve of mothers (whether or not they are working) putting small children in a day care center.
      Strongly agree ............................................. 1    [12]
      Agree ........................................................ 2
      Disagree .................................................... 3
      Strongly disagree ...................................... 4

172. If both husband and wife are working, they should split the housework 50-50.
      Strongly agree ............................................. 1    [13]
      Agree ........................................................ 2
      Disagree .................................................... 3
      Strongly disagree ...................................... 4

173. It is a mistake to have blacks for foremen and leaders over whites.
      Strongly agree ............................................. 1    [14]
      Agree ........................................................ 2
      Disagree .................................................... 3
      Strongly disagree ...................................... 4

174. Obedience and respect for authority are the most important virtues children should learn.
      Strongly agree ............................................. 1    [15]
      Agree ........................................................ 2
      Disagree .................................................... 3
      Strongly disagree ...................................... 4

175. There is nothing wrong in paying women less than men for doing similar work when they are not the major "breadwinners" in the family
      Strongly agree ............................................. 1    [16]
      Agree ........................................................ 2
      Disagree .................................................... 3
      Strongly disagree ...................................... 4

176. It is sometimes justifiable for a man and woman to have sexual relations outside marriage.
      Strongly agree ............................................. 1    [17]
      Agree ........................................................ 2
      Disagree .................................................... 3
      Strongly disagree ...................................... 4

177. In marriage, it's the man who should make the important decisions.
      Strongly agree ............................................. 1    [18]
      Agree ........................................................ 2
      Disagree .................................................... 3
      Strongly disagree ...................................... 4

178. I would not like to have a woman as my boss or superior on a job.

Strongly agree .............................................. 1    [19]
Agree .......................................................... 2
Disagree ...................................................... 3
Strongly disagree ........................................ 4

179. It is the duty of a citizen to criticize or censure his country whenever he considers it to be wrong.

Strongly agree .............................................. 1    [20]
Agree .......................................................... 2
Disagree ...................................................... 3
Strongly disagree ........................................ 4

180. An insult to your honor should not be forgotten.

Strongly agree .............................................. 1    [21]
Agree .......................................................... 2
Disagree ...................................................... 3
Strongly disagree ........................................ 4

181. It is only natural and right that women should have less freedom than men.

Strongly agree .............................................. 1    [22]
Agree .......................................................... 2
Disagree ...................................................... 3
Strongly disagree ........................................ 4

182. Women should stay out of politics.

Strongly agree .............................................. 1    [23]
Agree .......................................................... 2
Disagree ...................................................... 3
Strongly disagree ........................................ 4

183. A few strong leaders could make this country better than all the laws and talk.

Strongly agree .............................................. 1    [24]
Agree .......................................................... 2
Disagree ...................................................... 3
Strongly disagree ........................................ 4

184. Most people who don't get ahead just don't have enough will power.

Strongly agree .............................................. 1    [25]
Agree .......................................................... 2
Disagree ...................................................... 3
Strongly disagree ........................................ 4

**X.** In this section we are interested in your participation in organizations other than your local church.

185. Please look at the examples of various types of organizations below, then tell how many organizations of each type you participate in. (Enter in the space in front of each type the number of organizations of that type you participate in. If you belong to no organizations of a particular type, enter a 0. If you belong to no organizations at all, go to question 195.)

____VETERANS, MILITARY AND PATRIOTIC    [26-27]
ORGANIZATIONS such as American Legion, VFW, Disabled Veterans, D.A.R., AMVETS, Goldstar Mothers, etc.

____ORGANIZATIONS RELATING TO HEALTH    [28-29]
(EXCEPT SICK BENEFIT ASSOCIATIONS) such as Hospital board, Red Cross, American Cancer Society, March of Dimes, County Medical Society, Handicap Club, Registered Nurses Foundation, Nurses' Aid Club, etc.

____CIVIC OR SERVICE ORGANIZATIONS    [30-31]
such as Lions, Kiwanis, Rotary, Chamber of Commerce, Community Chest, Junior League, Boy Scouts, School Board member, PTA, etc.

____POLITICAL OR PRESSURE GROUPS    [32-33]
such as League of Women Voters, Democratic or Republican Party, Americans for Democratic Action, etc.

____LODGES, FRATERNAL SECRET SOCIETIES,    [34-35]
and MUTUAL (SICK) BENEFIT ASSOCIATIONS such as Masons, Elks, Moose, Shrine, Sons of Italy, Knights of Pythias, etc.

____CHURCH, RELIGIOUS ORGANIZATIONS    [36-37]
such as American Bible Society, Women's Home and Foreign Mission, Luther League, Men's Club at Church, etc.

____ECONOMIC, OCCUPATIONAL OR PRO-    [38-39]
FESSIONAL ORGANIZATIONS such as Merchants and Manufacturers Club, Truck Drivers Association, American Bar Association, AMA, Farm Bureau, etc.

____CULTURAL, EDUCATIONAL, COLLEGE    [40-41]
ALUMNI such as Museum Board, Lecture Club, Literary Club, Symphony Orchestra Board, Association for family living, etc.

____SOCIAL, SPORTS, HOBBY, OR RECREA-    [42-43]
TIONAL ORGANIZATIONS such as Country Club, Bridge Club, Camera Club, Flower Club, Boating League, Homemakers Club, etc.

186. Now we want to ask you a series of questions about the one organization (other than your church) which you feel is of the greatest importance to you personally. (Write full name of the organization which is *most*    [44-45] important to you personally.)

187. Listed below are several reasons often given by people when they are asked why they participate in organizations. Please indicate the three reasons which you feel are *important* for your own participation in this particular organization.

Enter here the number of the *one* reason
which *best* explains your participation ............____    [46-47]

Enter here the number in front of the reason
which is *second* in importance in your own
participation ................................................____    [48-49]

Enter here the number in front of the reason
which is *third* in importance in your own
participation ................................................____    [50-51]

01  This organization gives me a means of helping those in need (such as the sick, aged, lonely, or bereaved)
02  It's the expected thing to do in our community
03  Participating in the organization is just plain fun
04  I participate out of force of habit
05  It's good for business
06  It's a good way to meet people
07  It's the best way to serve God
08  My spouse wants me to participate
09  It is a way of exerting influence on the community to provide opportunity and justice for all its citizens
10  It's a requirement for my job
11  It gives me an opportunity to help young people
12  It gives me a means of contributing to the solution of social problems
13  My friends want me to participate
14  It's a means of seeking better government
15  It gives me a chance to associate with the most influential people in the community

188. In an average month about how much time do you devote to this organization?
- Less than an hour .......................................... 1   [52]
- 1 or 2 hours ................................................. 2
- 3 or 4 hours ................................................. 3
- 5 hours or more ........................................... 4

189. For how many years have you been active in this organization?
- Less than a year .......................................... 1   [53]
- 1 or 2 years ................................................ 2
- 3 or 4 years ................................................ 3
- 5 years or more ........................................... 4

190. Compared to the average member, would you say you were
- More active ................................................. 1   [54]
- Less active ................................................. 2
- About the same ........................................... 3

191. Have you ever held an office in this organization?
- Yes ............................................................ 1   [55]
- No ............................................................. 2

IF YES
191a. What is the highest office you have held?
- President ..................................................... 1   [56]
- Vice President ............................................. 2
- Secretary or treasurer .................................. 3
- Committee chairman .................................... 4
- Committee member ...................................... 5
- Other .......................................................... 6

192. Do you think it's right for this organization to take actions on political and social action issues?
- Yes ............................................................ 1   [57]
- No ............................................................. 2
- Sometimes .................................................. 3

193. Has this organization ever taken a public stand on controversial political or social issues?
- Yes ............................................................ 1   [58]
- No ............................................................. 2

IF YES
193a. Has it done this
- Once ........................................................... 1   [59]
- Occasionally ............................................... 2
- Frequently .................................................. 3
193b. What controversial issues has the organization most recently taken a stand on?
                                              [60-61]
193c. Have you ever directly taken part in any of these political or social action activities in the organization?
- Yes ............................................................ 1   [62]
- No ............................................................. 2
IF YES
193d. Have you done this
- Once ........................................................... 1   [63]
- Twice .......................................................... 2
- More than that ............................................ 3
193e. How often do you agree with the stands taken by the organization on such issues? Would you say
- Never .......................................................... 1   [64]
- Rarely ......................................................... 2
- Sometimes .................................................. 3
- Usually ....................................................... 4
- Almost always ............................................. 5

194a. Of *all* the organizations you belong to (*excluding the church*), which one would you say has the most influence on your attitudes toward social issues?
                                              [65-66]

194b. Compared with the organization just indicated, would you say that the church has more, less, or about the same influence on your attitudes toward social issues?
- More ........................................................... 1   [67]
- Less ............................................................ 2
- About the same ........................................... 3

Here are some questions about politics.

195. Which political party do you prefer?
- Republican .................................................. 1   [68]
- Democrat .................................................... 2
- Independent ................................................ 3
- Wallace's American Independent Party ........ 4
- Other .......................................................... 5
- No preference ............................................. 6

196. If a group of people in this country strongly feels that they are being treated unfairly, what kinds of actions do you think they have the right to take in trying to change the situation? Listed below are different kinds of actions that dissatisfied groups sometimes take. After each action, please indicate whether or not you think dissatisfied groups have the right to do this.

a. Take actions such as either boycotting or getting up a petition.
- No .............................................................. 1   [69]
- Yes ............................................................ 2
b. Hold public speeches and rallies
- No .............................................................. 1   [70]
- Yes ............................................................ 2
c. Stage mass demonstrations with large crowds of people.
- No .............................................................. 1   [71]
- Yes ............................................................ 2
d. Engage in civil disobedience by breaking laws which are considered unjust.
- No .............................................................. 1   [72]
- Yes ............................................................ 2
e. Take actions such as "sit-ins" or "walk-outs".
- No .............................................................. 1   [73]
- Yes ............................................................ 2
f. March quietly and peacefully through town.
- No .............................................................. 1   [74]
- Yes ............................................................ 2

XI. This final brief section asks some questions about your personal background.
                              [731..................07]

197. How old were you on your last birthday?
- 11 years or younger .................................... 1   [10]
- 12-17 .......................................................... 2
- 18-24 .......................................................... 3
- 25-30 .......................................................... 4
- 31-49 .......................................................... 5
- 50-65 .......................................................... 6
- 66-75 .......................................................... 7
- 76 or older .................................................. 8

198. Are you
- Male ........................................................... 1   [11]
- Female ........................................................ 2

199. Are you
- White ......................................................... 1   [12]
- Black .......................................................... 2
- Other (please specify) ................................. 3

200. Which income group (below) includes your *total family income* before taxes in 1972, considering all sources such as wages, rents, profits, and interests?

| $ | 0- 2,999 | | 01 [13-14] |
|---|---|---|---|

$ 0- 2,999 ................................... 01 [13-14]
 3,000- 4,999 ................................... 02
 5,000- 6,999 ................................... 03
 7,000- 8,999 ................................... 04
 9,000-10,999 ................................... 05
11,000-12,999 ................................... 06
13,000-14,999 ................................... 07
15,000-19,999 ................................... 08
20,000-24,999 ...................................09
25,000-29,999 ................................... 10
30,000-39,999 ................................... 11
40,000-49,999 ................................... 12
50,000 and over ..................... 13

201. Using the job categories printed below, please enter the number following the one job category which comes closest to the type of job the following persons in your family hold (or held before retirement or death).

A. CURRENT HEAD OF HOUSEHOLD

———— [15-16]

B. SPOUSE (But if your spouse is the current head of your household, print the number 88 here)

———— [17-18]

C. FATHER (But if your father is the current head of your household, print the number 88 here)

———— [19-20]

D. YOURSELF (But if you are the current head of your household, please print the number 88 here)

———— [21-22]

BUSINESS AND GOVERNMENT
a. Owners, managers, and administrators—such as owner of a business, building contractor, office manager, sales manager, banker, school administrator, military officer, etc. ................ 01
b. Clerical—such as bank teller, bookkeeper, secretary, typist, office machine operator, cashier, mail carrier, etc. ................................... 02
c. Sales—such as salesman, sales clerk, etc ......... 03

FACTORY AND NONINDUSTRIAL WORKERS
a. Technician—such as medical or dental technician, computer programmer, draftsman, etc ................................... 04
b. Craftsman—such as machinist, toolmaker, diemaker, electrician, plumber, carpenter, brickmason, welder, etc. ................................... 05
c. Operative—such as machine operator in a factory, assembler, truck driver, automobile mechanic, etc. ................................... 06
d. Laborer—such as car washer, carpenter's helper, sanitary worker, janitor, construction laborer, etc. ................................... 07

PROFESSIONAL
a. Professional I—such as medical doctor, dentist, lawyer, judge, architect, scientist, college professor, etc. ................................... 08

b. Professional II—such as engineer, accountant, teacher, librarian, registered nurse, social worker, clergyman, etc. ................................... 09

SERVICE
a. Personal Service—such as barber, beautician, practical nurse, waiter, etc. ................................... 10
b. Domestic Service—such as maid, cook, etc. .... 11
c. Protective Service—such as policeman, detective, guard, sherriff, fireman, etc. ................................... 12

FARMER, FARM MANAGER ................ 13

HOMEMAKER OR HOUSEWIFE ................ 14

STUDENT ................................... 15

202. How many years of school did you complete?
 0-8 years ................................... 01 [23-24]
 9-11 (some high school) ................................... 02
 12 (high school graduate) ................................... 03
 12+ business or technical school after high school ................................... 04
 13-15 (some college) ................................... 05
 16 (college graduate) ................................... 06
 17 or more (grad work after college degree) ................................... 07

IF MARRIED
203. How many years of school has your wife/husband completed?
 0-8 years ................................... 01 [25-26]
 9-11 (some high school) ................................... 02
 12 (high school graduate) ................................... 03
 12+ business or technical school after high school ................................... 04
 13-15 (some college) ................................... 05
 16 (college graduate) ................................... 06
 17 or more (grad work after college degree) ................................... 07

204. Are you presently single, married, widowed, divorced, or separated?
 Single ................................... 1 [27]
 Married ................................... 2
 Widowed ................................... 3
 Divorced ................................... 4
 Separated ................................... 5

205. How many years have you lived in the Indianapolis area?
 Less than a year ................................... 1 [28]
 One to five years ................................... 2
 Six to ten years ................................... 3
 More than ten years ................................... 4

206. Were you born in Indiana?
 Yes ................................... 1 [29]
 No ................................... 2
IF NO
206a. In what state (or foreign country) were you born?
 [30-31]

Thank you very much for completing the questionnaire. We sincerely appreciate your help.

Please remember to mail the post card (attached at the center of the questionnaire) as well as the questionnaire. (No message is necessary on the post card; its number will tell us you have responded).

This space has been left for any comments you would like to make.

# References

Almond, Gabriel A. and Sidney Verba
    1963 The Civic Culture. Princeton: Princeton University Press.
Barber, Bernard
    1950 "Participation and mass apathy in associations." Pages
        477–504 in A. W. Gouldner (ed.), Studies in Leadership. New
        York: Harper and Brothers.
Barnard, Chester
    1966 The Functions of the Executive. Cambridge, Mass.: Harvard
        University Press.
Barton, Allen H.
    1961 Organizational Measurement. New York: College Entrance
        Examination Board.
Bellah, Robert N.
    1967 "Civil religion in America." Daedalus 96(Winter): 1–21.
Berger, Peter L.
    1963 "Charisma and religious innovation: the social location of Is-
        raelite prophecy." American Sociological Review
        28(December): 940–950.
Berger, Peter L. and Thomas Luckmann
    1966 The Social Construction of Reality. Garden City, N.Y.:
        Doubleday.
Bierstedt, Robert
    1954 "The problem of authority." Pages 67–81 in Monroe Berger,
        Theodore Abel, and Charles H. Page (eds.), Freedom and Con-
        trol in Modern Society. Princeton: Van Nostrand.
Blaikie, Norman W.
    1976 "The use of 'denomination' in sociological explanation: the
        case of the position of clergy on social issues." Journal for the
        Scientific Study of Religion 15(March): 79–86.

Blau, Peter M.
    1964 Exchange and Power in Social Life. New York: John Wiley
        and Sons.
Blau, Peter M. and Richard Schoenherr
    1971 The Structure of Organizations. New York: Basic Books.
Blau, Peter M. and W. Richard Scott
    1962 Formal Organizations. San Francisco: Chandler.
Bohrnstedt, George W.
    1966 Processes of Seeking Membership in and Recruitment by Vol-
        untary Social Organizations. Ph.D. dissertation, University of
        Wisconsin.
Buckley, Walter
    1967 Sociology and Modern Systems Theory. Englewood Cliffs,
        N.J.: Prentice-Hall.
Burns, James MacGregor
    1978 Leadership. New York: Harper and Row.
Burton, Joe W.
    1965 Annual of the Southern Baptist Convention. Nashville, Tenn.:
        Executive Committee, Southern Baptist Convention.
Burton, Malcolm K.
    1953 Destiny for Congregationalism. Oklahoma City: Modern
        Publishers.
Campbell, Ernest Q. and Thomas F. Pettigrew
    1959 Christians in Racial Crisis. Washington, D.C.: Public Affairs
        Press.
Clark, Peter B. and James Q. Wilson
    1961 "Incentive systems: a theory of organizations." Administrative
        Science Quarterly 6(September): 129–166.
Coleman, James S.
    1957 Community Conflict. Glencoe, Ill.: Free Press.
Cowan, Edward
    1976 "Teamsters group seeks to curb leaders power." Louisville
        Courier Journal (May 28): A 8.
Durkheim, Emile
    1964 The Rules of Sociological Method. New York: Free Press.
Edelman, Murray
    1971 Politics as Symbolic Action. Chicago: Markham.
Elder, Glen H., Jr.
    1975 "Age differentiation and the life course." Annual Review of So-
        ciology 1: 165–190.

Etzioni, Amitai
　　1961 A Comparative Analysis of Complex Organizations. New York:
　　　　Free Press.
　　1968 The Active Society. New York: Free Press.
Feagin, Joe R.
　　1975 Subordinating the Poor: Welfare and American Beliefs. Lex-
　　　　ington, Mass.: Lexington Books.
Fiske, Edward B.
　　1970 "Protestant churches cut staffs as support drops." New York
　　　　Times (March 31).
Gamson, William A.
　　1968 Power and Discontent. Homewood, Ill.: Dorsey Press.
Glock, Charles Y. and Rodney Stark
　　1966 Christian Beliefs and Anti-Semitism. New York: Harper and
　　　　Row.
Gouldner, Alvin W.
　　1955 "Metaphysical pathos and the theory of bureaucracy." Ameri-
　　　　can Political Science Review 49(June): 496–507.
Greer, Scott A.
　　1955 Social Organization. New York: Random House.
Hadden, Jeffrey K.
　　1969 The Gathering Storm in the Churches. Garden City, N.Y.:
　　　　Doubleday.
Hadden, Jeffrey K. and Charles F. Longino, Jr.
　　1974 Gideon's Gang: A Case Study of the Church in Social Action.
　　　　Philadelphia: United Church Press.
Harrison, Paul M.
　　1959 Authority and Power in the Free Church Tradition. Princeton:
　　　　Princeton University Press.
Heider, Fritz
　　1946 "Attitudes and cognitive organization." Journal of Psychology
　　　　21: 107–112.
Hill, Michael
　　1973 The Religious Order. London: Heinemann.
Hirschman, Albert O.
　　1970 Exit, Voice, and Loyalty. Cambridge, Mass.: Harvard Univer-
　　　　sity Press.
Hoge, Dean R.
　　1976 Division in the Protestant House. Philadelphia: Westminster
　　　　Press.

International Labor Office
  1974 Yearbook of Labor Statistics. Geneva: International Labor
       Office.
Jenkins, J. Craig and Charles Perrow
  1977 "Insurgency of the powerless: farm worker movements
       (1946–1972)." American Sociological Review 42(April):
       249–268.
Johnson, Douglas W. and George W. Cornell
  1972 Punctured Preconceptions. New York: Friendship Press.
Kelley, Dean M.
  1972 Why Conservative Churches Are Growing. New York: Harper
       and Row.
Knoke, David H. and James R. Wood
  1981 Organized for Action: Commitment in Voluntary Associations.
       New Brunswick, N.J.: Rutgers University Press.
Kornhauser, William
  1959 The Politics of Mass Society. Glencoe, Ill.: Free Press.
LaPiere, Richard
  1954 A Theory of Social Control. New York: McGraw-Hill.
Lazarsfeld, Paul F., Ann K. Pananella, and Morris Rosenberg (eds.)
  1972 Continuities in the Language of Social Research. New York:
       Free Press.
Lenski, Gerhard
  1963 The Religious Factor. Garden City, N.Y.: Doubleday.
Lichtenberger, Arthur
  1964 "The presiding bishop's special fund." Church and Race
       1(April–May): 14–15.
Linz, Juan
  1968 "Michels, Robert." Pages 265–272 in David L. Sills (ed.), In-
       ternational Encyclopedia of the Social Sciences. New York:
       Macmillan and Free Press.
Lipset, Seymour M.
  1950 Agrarian Socialism. Berkeley: University of California Press.
  1960 Political Man. Garden City, N.Y.: Doubleday.
  1962 "Introduction." In Robert Michels, Political Parties. New York:
       Free Press.
Lipset, Seymour M., Martin Trow, and James Coleman
  1962 Union Democracy. Garden City, N.Y.: Doubleday.
Mannheim, Karl
  1952 Essays on the Sociology of Knowledge. London: Routledge
       and Kegan Paul.

Mayer, Allan J., John J. Lindsay, Howard Fineman, Stryker McGuire, Jonathan Kirsch, and Michael Reese
1980 "A Tide of Born-Again Politics." Newsweek (September 15): 28–36.

Merton, Robert K.
1957 Social Theory and Social Structure. Glencoe, Ill.: Free Press.

Merton, Robert K., George G. Reader, and Patricia L. Kendall
1957 The Student-physician: Introductory Studies in the Sociology of Medical Education. Cambridge: Mass.: Harvard University Press.

Michels, Robert
1962 Political Parties. New York: Free Press.

Moberg, David
1964 The Church as a Social Institution. Englewood Cliffs, N.J.: Prentice-Hall.

Moore, G. H. and J. N. Hedges
1971 "Trends in labor and leisure." Monthly Labor Review 94: 3–11.

Myrdal, Gunnar, et al.
1963 An American Dilemma: The Negro Problem and Modern Democracy. New York: Harper and Row.

Nagel, Ernest
1961 The Structure of Science. New York: Harcourt Brace World.

National Council, Protestant Episcopal Church
1963 "Statement of policy with regard to race." Adopted December 1963. (Mimeographed)

Niebuhr, H. Richard
1951 Christ and Culture. New York: Harper and Brothers.
1956 The Purpose of the Church and Its Ministry. New York: Harper and Brothers.

A. C. Nielsen Company
1979 Nielsen National TV Ratings (November 12–25): 11–12. New York: A. C. Nielsen Company.

Nisbet, Robert
1970 The Social Bond. New York: Alfred A. Knopf.

Olsen, Marvin E. and Mary Anna Baden
1974 "Legitimacy of social protest action in the United States and Sweden." Journal of Political and Military Sociology 2(Fall): 173–189.

Olson, Mancur, Jr.
1968 The Logic of Collective Action. New York: Shocken.

Owen, George Earle (ed.)
  1972 1972 Year Book and Directory. Indianapolis: General Office of
    the Christian Church (Disciples of Christ).
Pratt, Henry J.
  1972 The Liberalization of American Protestantism. Detroit: Wayne
    State University Press.
Quinley, Harold E.
  1974a "The dilemma of an activist church: Protestant religion in
    the sixties and seventies." Journal for the Scientific Study of
    Religion 13(March): 1–21.
  1974b The Prophetic Clergy: Social Activism among Protestant
    Ministers. New York: John Wiley and Sons.
Rappaport, Roy A.
  1971 "The sacred in human evolution." Annual Review of Ecology
    and Systematics 2:23–44.
  1979 Ecology, Meaning, and Religion. Richmond, Calif.: North
    Atlantic.
Roe, Betty Boyd and James R. Wood
  1975 "Adaptive innovation and organizational security." Pacific So-
    ciological Review 18(July):310–326.
Rokeach, Milton
  1973 The Nature of Human Values. New York: Free Press.
Satow, Roberta Lynn
  1975 "Value-rational authority and professional organizations:
    Weber's missing type." Administrative Science Quarterly
    20(December):526–531.
Schmidt, Alvin J.
  1973 Oligarchy in Fraternal Organizations. Detroit: Gale Research
    Company.
Selznick, Philip
  1957 Leadership in Administration. New York: Harper and Row.
Shupe, Anson D., Jr., and James R. Wood
  1973 "Sources of leadership ideology in dissident clergy." Sociologi-
    cal Analysis (Fall):185–201.
Simon, Herbert A.
  1965 Administrative Behavior. New York: Free Press.
Spike, Robert W.
  1965 The Freedom Revolution and the Churches. New York: Asso-
    ciation Press.
Spock, Benjamin M.
  1946 The Common Sense Book of Baby and Child Care. New York:
    Duell, Sloan and Pearce.

Stinchcombe, Arthur L.
   1968 Constructing Social Theories. New York: Harcourt, Brace and World.
Stouffer, Samuel A.
   1963 Communism, Conformity, and Civil Liberties. Gloucester, Mass.: Peter Smith.
Tagiuri, Renato and George H. Litwin (eds.)
   1968 Organizational Climate. Boston: Graduate School of Business Administration, Harvard University.
Taylor, Mary G.
   1975 "Two models of social reform action in a normative organization." Sociological Analysis 36(Summer): 161–167.
Thomas, Cal
   1980 "Nation's moral tailspin reflects church apathy." Moral Majority Report 1(September 15): 4–5.
Turner, Ralph H. and Lewis M. Killian
   1972 Collective Behavior. Englewood Cliffs, N.J.: Prentice-Hall.
U.S. Bureau of the Census
   1975 Historical Statistics of the United States: Colonial Times to 1970. Bicentennial Edition. Washington, D.C.: U.S. Bureau of the Census.
Wallace, Walter L. (ed.)
   1969 Sociological Theory. Chicago: Aldine.
Weber, Max
   1968 Economy and Society. Edited by Guenther Roth and Claus Wittich. New York: Bedminister Press.
Will, George F.
   1976 "Taking a ride with Ronnie." Newsweek 87(May 31): 76.
Willer, David E.
   1967 "Max Weber's missing authority type." Sociological Inquiry 37: 231–239.
Wood, James R.
   1967 Protestant Enforcement of Racial Integration Policy: A Sociological Study in the Political Economy of Organizations. Ph.D. dissertation, Vanderbilt University.
   1970 "Authority and controversial policy: the churches and civil rights." American Sociological Review 35(December): 1057–1069.
   1972a "Personal commitment and organizational constraint: church officials and racial integration." Sociological Analysis 33(Fall): 142–151.
   1972b "Unanticipated consequences of organizational coalitions:

     ecumenical cooperation and civil rights policy." Social Forces 50(June): 512–521.

  1975 "Legitimate control and 'organizational transcendence.'" Social Forces 54(September): 199–211.

Wood, James R. and Mayer N. Zald

  1966 "Aspects of racial integration in the Methodist Church: sources of resistance to organizational policy." Social Forces 45(December): 255–265.

Zald, Mayer N. and Roberta Ash

  1966 "Social movement organizations: growth, decay and change." Social Forces 44(March): 327–341.

Zald, Mayer N. and Patricia Denton

  1963 "From evangelism to general service: the transformation of the YMCA." Administrative Science Quarterly 8(September): 214–234.

# Index